ABOUT THE AUTHOR

J.K Sheindlin is the author of the controversial #1 international bestseller *'The People vs Muhammad - Psychological Analysis'*, which has been critically praised, and considered the most dangerous book written since the turn of the millennium.

Sheindlin is a passionate contributor to the fight against injustice and the growing threat of universal censorship. The author has spent years researching the true origins of Islam and has fervently documented the rise of Islamization in western countries. Recently, Sheindlin has come under attack by the social media elite for the unflinching truth contained with each book published.

'The People vs Muhammad - Psychological Analysis', has been set to be banned and censored by the Canadian Federation of Library Associations, for being 'too dangerous' to read. At the same time, and not surprisingly, it has been banned in the Arab states, and now on Amazon India. Nonetheless, despite the echelon's desperate attempts to silence the truth, the book series remains on the international bestseller lists in 'Religious studies' and 'Religion, State and Politics':

#1 in USA
#1 in UK
#1 in Canada
#1 in Germany

To verify these records, you can visit the author's website and watch the video '5 star reviews'.

The critically acclaimed success of the book series is attributed to the unprecedented work Sheindlin pioneered in psychologically deconstructing Muhammad, which is the first time in history anyone has critically analysed the man's psyche, his sexual habits, and psychopathy. Perhaps the most startling revelation, is the fact that Muhammad most probably was afflicted with syphilis, which in turn evolved into neuro-syphilis, finally manifesting into paranoid schizophrenia. It is from this sexually transmitted disease which undoubtedly gave birth to Islam, and its eccentric tenets. Sheindlin has made numerous academic references to prove the case - no-one has been able to refute the truth.

Sheindlin's second bestseller *'Questions that Islam can't answer'* also proves to be an invaluable tool in waking up Muslims to the truth. The contents of this book serves to be a testing tool for Muslims who obstinately refuse to accept the truth, and wilfully continue to engage in the same depraved acts as their master.

'Censored' is the explosive tell-all autobiography from #1 international bestseller J.K Sheindlin, the critically acclaimed author of 'The People vs Muhammad - Psychological Analysis', and 'Questions that Islam can't answer'.

Persecuted by Big Tech and reviled by the liberal elites, Sheindlin is the ultimate insider to global censorship who dared to psychoanalyse the founder of the world's most intolerable religion. After popular demand, the author finally shares the controversial story.

Driven from the social media landscape, and labeled as persona-non-grata in the emerging globalist world, Sheindlin unveils the dirty communist tactics used by Big Tech to intimidate, crush and censor opponents of the liberal-Marxist agenda.

In this book, you will…

- *Be informed firsthand from the insider's experience.*
- *Learn how the tech elites broke their own rules in desperation to kill the author's exposure.*
- *Discover how Big Tech historically aided in creating the holocaust, and the formation of the European political superstate.*
- *Be warned about the master plan Silicon Valley is ushering in to silence your speech, and how the industry protects pedophiles but punishes patriots.*
- *Learn how the CIA created the global censorship and media manipulation program today known as Project Mockingbird.*
- *Find out how Obama became the catalyst to bring the west to its knees.*
- *Discover how Obama's mother's CIA family history has infiltrated the tech industry to usher in communism.*
- *Witness leaked documents and sources showing liberal infiltration of Big Tech.*
- *Find out how even the mainstream churches have been infiltrated.*
- *Be aware of how each of the bill of rights have been violated.*
- *Learn how to protect your rights and to resist global censorship.*

A timely and erudite release due to the increase of draconian online censorship, J.K Sheindlin is the harbinger for humanity, and brings a warning to all of the coming global persecution complex.

CENSORED

WRITTEN BY

J.K SHEINDLIN

For all information about this author, visit:

www.jksheindlin.com

CONTENTS

FOREWORD   8

DEDICATION AND REMEMBRANCE   11

THE CANARY IN THE COAL MINE   15

HOW MY JOURNEY BEGAN   17

THE TRUTH SETS THE CAPTIVES FREE   28

THE CENSORSHIP BEGINS   33

FACEBOOK CENSORS ME   36

TWITTER CENSORS ME   42

GOOGLE CENSORS ME   47

YOUTUBE CENSORS ME   54

BARNES AND NOBLE CENSORS MY REVIEWERS   85

DISQUS CENSORS ME   86

THE CANADIAN FEDERATION OF LIBRARY ASSOCIATIONS CENSORS ME   88

MY FIGHT WITH DISTRIBUTION COMPANIES   90

THE WAR ON FREEDOM   92

THE DIABOLICAL SYSTEM OF CONTROL   96

THE CREATION OF A POLICE STATE   99

THE BIGGEST CENSORSHIP SCANDAL IN HISTORY   101

THE BRAINWASHING MACHINE   106

THE LIBERAL YOUTH INHERIT THE FUTURE   115

THE HITLER-LIBERAL ALLIANCE   127

THE GOOD CENSOR   131

THEY WHO WANT TO KILL US   144

OUR BLEAK FUTURE   153

OVERRULED BRITANNIA   155

EUROMEGALOMANIA   161

THEY WILL BREAK YOU   165

RULED BY FOOLS   168

THE END IS NIGH   173

THE DEATH OF LIBERTY   178

THE VOICE OF REASON   193

PLAN OF ACTION   195

FIGHT BIG TECH WITH CLASSIFICATION LAWS   196

SUPPORT STRICTER CITIZENSHIP LAWS   200

KNOW YOUR RIGHTS AND THE LAW   204

SPEAK THE TRUTH AND BE INDEPENDENT   211

GET COMMUNICATING   214

KNOW THY ENEMY   215

OPPOSE NEO-COMMUNISM AND THE SHARIA   216

MY FINAL WORDS   219

THE ELEVENTH HOUR   223

AS I PUT MY PEN DOWN   225

FOREWORD

We are under attack. Not from external forces, but from within our own civilisation. We are now facing an old enemy today which was introduced by the soviet union to cripple our core beliefs. That enemy is called political correctness. It is a pernicious, cancerous disease which has infected the minds of the liberal left by their delusional overlords, who revel in turning our world into a technocratic, dictatorial, dystopia based on the principles of cultural Marxism.

I wrote this book, not as a rant, a whinge, but as a warning to all. If they came for me, they will soon come for you. As a champion of truth, justice and the American way, I have been rampantly persecuted and silenced for daring to speak up against the beast. My quest and ultimate censorship has all been documented in this book as a referenced testimony and harbinger to all who believe that they are indemnified against persecution through silence. You're not.

While the uneducated leftist world dances, and imbibes mind-numbing garbage, fed by the globalist elite, like many others I have been going through living hell, all while the populous sleep soundly in their beds, believing that tomorrow's freedoms are guaranteed.

There is a silent genocide of intellectualism and truism occurring. Those who have took up the mantle to protect our freedoms have been proverbially seized in secret during the night, and faced no trial, but a swift ruling to be purged from the online community for where our entire lives are now invested.

As the author of the book which has turned many Muslims away from the cult known as Islam, I've been ex-communicated on all social media networks, and have received the eternal mark to be blacklisted, and written out of the technocrats capricious book of life.

While many will believe that the tone in this book will be very harsh and unbecoming of a Christian, I myself make no apologies for this. The gloves are off. The liberal elites have played dirty for far too long, and it's time to fight back with the truth, no matter how unpalatable it is, or how critical I will be. Truth is truth, it has no filter. The lord Jesus Christ warned us that we could not serve two masters. A line has been drawn in the sand. He who will come again, came before to divide the world with a sword, between truth and the lie. It is up to you to make your decision for the light, or the darkness.

But for how long will this age of tyranny last?

The answer lies in how long you as a citizen of a free nation will tolerate it. Your mandate as a created being bestowed with the gift of reason, consciousness and the inherent sense of free-will, have the choice to accept the path laid to hell by the globalist elite, or to reject it.

If you seek the light, the truth, then they will come for you, like they came for me.

Be warned.

"People hate the truth for the sake of whatever it is that they love more than the truth. They love truth when it shines warmly on them, and hate it when it rebukes them."

- St Augustine of Hippo

DEDICATION AND REMEMBRANCE

Apart from the fact that conservatives are being rampantly targeted in the west, we seem to forget that a silent persecution continues everyday around the world. For the millions of Christians who have been murdered by Islamic regimes, my hearts and prayers go out to you. Indeed, the world has forgotten your plight, which disgusts me. We have all abandoned our duty to seek justice for you and the family you've lost. It breaks my heart to say that while you were being raped, tortured, robbed, and murdered, the world carried on like it was just another normal day; as if genocide and ethnic cleansing was an intrinsic part of our DNA. If it wasn't, our governments would have stepped in a long time ago to rescue you. They didn't, and you've had to pay the price for their ungodly ways. To add insult to the indignity you have faced, our corrupt governments not only have neglected you, but have allowed those who have murdered and raped your families to return back home without any prosecution for crimes against humanity. This is something that I still cannot come to terms with.

It's evident that as each day passes, you were born on the wrong side of history. Your religion rejects abortions, and believes in the sanctity of human life. You believe in good will, charity and loving your enemy. Therefore, you've become an inconvenience to the Satanic establishment, for whom total culpability rests upon. But it doesn't matter to them. The fact that you even existed, is an insult to the average liberal. It wasn't because you were out of sight, or lived thousands of miles away. It was because you are a *Christian*, and the world couldn't care less about you. Our governments are more concerned with keeping up appearances, selling arms to radical Islamic regimes, and protecting the 'dignity' of Muslims back home; the same people who have called for the beheading of apostates and Christians in our own countries.

While there's no secret that our governments indirectly created murderous Islamic regimes with American taxpayer's money, it is our faith in the church which has become shattered because of its negligence to help Christians. Hardly any mention of Islamic atrocities towards minorities in the middle-east and other countries were ever mentioned by the church, or even conservative media. It's all been swept under the rug for the sake of political correctness. It's undeniable that you've been sold out for liberal values, as our now ecumenical church laughs, eats, drinks with, and pats their Taqiyya-practicing Muslim counterparts on the back. Meanwhile somewhere in the middle-east, a child was getting her head cut off, or being raped by a Muslim until there was nothing more to her; all for being a Christian. We all saw the images of the carnage left behind by ISIS, but the world just went back to spinning, and the church, laughing like a debauched fat pig.

It's an inescapable fact that such atrocities were unmentioned by the church who forgot you, as to preserve 'dialogue' with their 'Muslim brothers and sisters'. Today, the Christian population in whole parts of the middle-east is all but gone through Islam's program for ethnic cleansing. For those reading this who represented such churches, I say *shame on you!* You've lined your coffers while the people you swore to protect were begging for their help. I ask you to close your eyes and imagine what it would feel like to have your head slowly cut off, knowing that the church that you were faithful to, abandoned you to your death, all for political correctness.

For everyone else reading this, it is a harsh reality that the leaders we looked to for guidance and solidarity with the meek, all shirked their responsibilities, opting to invest in fickle trendy sexual politics and LGBT mania - all to stay in the loop with the hipsters and liberal mobsters. The term 'equality', and the modern woman's complaint over unfair treatment in the world is, in my opinion, crap. Not once have I seen any liberal protest over the misogynistic, brutal doctrines within the Quran. Miraculously, they're all silent as they know Islam is the untouchable sacred cow. Therefore, to such airheads, I say this. Try living under an oppressive Islamic regime as a woman, where your genitals are mutilated for 'cleanliness', you're routinely beaten, raped, and told you're going to hell regardless of your obsequiousness; all because you're a woman. Live just one day in those conditions, and then come to me with your liberal 'issues'. I doubt you would, because living in a close-minded, hermetic environment filled with perpetual confirmation bias, while riding on your high horse, is serving your liberal agenda. You don't care about women's rights, or the plight of Muslim women being abused in Islamic countries. All you care about is yourself.

Make no mistake, there will be a reckoning, a final judgment. All will kneel before a righteous God with an exceptionally long memory, to explain their wicked deeds. I pity those who will have to look in our Lord's eyes and explain how they filled their pockets with thirty pieces of silver, while their brothers and sisters were ravaged, tortured and murdered under their watch. The sun might have set on Islam's pseudo-caliphate, and its victims hastily buried in shallow graves, but I won't forget them. I know for a fact that they shall have justice in the next life, and all those in the west who conspired to shut down people like myself and many others who spoke the truth, will also face an almighty God.

> For we will all stand before God's judgment seat. It
> is written:
> "As surely as I live, says the Lord,
> every knee will bow before Me;
> every tongue will confess to God."
> So then, each of us will give an account of himself
> to God.
> Romans 14:10-12

THE CANARY IN THE COAL MINE

While we may believe we are still privileged to live in a society where free expression, consciousness and thought is cherished, in reality these are no longer afforded to those who seek to push the boundaries or challenge the cultural standardisation of falsehood. Moreover, neither are they considered virtuous by a growingly narcissistic youth who have taken the liberal cool-aid and seductive promises of world-wide control. As each day quickly passes, we are somewhat slowly becoming aware of the creeping dawn of a technological tyrannical age. But in truth, the average layman certainly does not realise that Marxism has become entrenched in our society... or how far the rot has set in. As an insider to the persistent battle conservatives and Christians face against the Goliath system of ideological oppression, I will divulge the most personal details of my journey, which will give you an idea of the fight I have engaged in while the public remained unaware. Like many who refuse to accept the big lie, I have emerged with the battle scars and a story which would make you sick to your stomach.

To those who may be wondering why my usual flamboyant book cover style has deviated to a more generic tone, the answer is quite simple. I have purposely designed this book cover to be as austere, bland, perfunctory and insipid as possible, for the main reason...

To alert people to the coming literary apocalypse and rise of communism in our western nations. It stands out because like the cancer that political correctness is, this is the only way I can wake people up. Take a good look at the cover again... this is how your future will look. Dead, cold, unimaginative, lest it offend. As you can see from any book retailer's listings, my book might stand out as the ugly duckling, and peculiarly incongruous, but this is only for a short while, as the culture of cyber-policing will create a vacuum of neo-book-burning and cultural conformity. Within time, books with such bland covers will no longer appear incongruous, but will fade into the crowd of soulless literary works, trampled down by the intolerant elite who walk on the skulls of martyrs and patriots.

We are now living in the preliminary stages of an overzealous, policed internet, where not only content is monitored, but the tone of expression. It's sad to say that our society has now officially lost itself, and has embraced an environment of academic intolerance, celebrated demagoguery, and a take-down culture based on personal grievances rather than merit. As a notice to all that don't heed my warning, if you believe that you are currently safe because you don't say anything that offends the establishment, think again. Your silence is not enough to please the demagogues who are already lining up to become the metaphysical principalities of this world. In Canada, freedom of speech has now officially come to an end. Bill C-16 states that silence implicates a citizen as an instrument of hate. The compulsion of speech is a concept that sees its roots formerly in the tyrannical days of the universal catechism. It's not enough to remain silent, but it will become mandatory to pledge allegiance to the system of deceit, and the corrupt rulers who are drunk with power.

A line has been drawn in the sand.

Do not make the mistake by remaining complacent. If they came for me, and the many others who have given their life for the truth, then they will come for you.

HOW MY JOURNEY BEGAN

Throughout the introduction in my first book, I divulged only a few key details into my life, and my fight. I purposely left out as much information as possible, not only for security reasons, but as not to detract from the subject at hand, which was Muhammad's mental disorders and the pertinence of a post-humous trial. My approach to the issue has always been through anonymity. The fact that I have remained anonymous for many years has perplexed many, and gained quite a negative stigma. It seems that the public today are not interested in merit, but only trivial personalities and the short-lived parlour tricks a one-minute wonder can perform. I attribute this to the cultural change our civilisation is facing today. Sadly, we have become a superficial nation where fame, celebrity and sensationalism has become more important than the message itself. It's also quite shocking that because of this, the national IQ average is also in decline. The globalist elites have worked tirelessly to pump as much garbage into our brains to disarm us from fighting back with academia, which is their enemy.

Unlike most authors, I did not slap a photo of myself on the cover to cash in on fame and celebrity like some self-promoting YouTuber or blogger. Indeed, celebrity commentators and journalists make the mistake of showing their face. In reality, it distracts from their merits. People can become so emotional and sidetracked simply by personality, yet fail to investigate further due to their own prejudices. With no image to attack, they have no target. They can only take aim at your words, but if they're sound, the globalists will resort to the only tactic left which remains, *censorship*.

The establishment has tried everything to derail my cause, but their efforts are futile. My name still has remained as an idea of change and challenge. You can kill the person, you can erase their identity, but you can't destroy the idea. An idea is a dangerous weapon. Once entered into the subject's brain, it will remain there forever. The person may suppress it deep within their cerebral cortex, but any trigger word, sound, action or phrase will one day inevitably induce the idea to the realm of conscience. This was ultimately my plan; to reach as many minds as possible, to counter global deceit. In truth, we are already embroiled in an information war. Unlike many agents of opportunity seeking to milk the Islamic problem to its last drop, I was never interested in the limelight, but only relished in reaching out to millions with the undiscovered truth which might had changed the world for the better. If that had indeed happened, I would have very easily walked away back into the shadows and carried on with my life. Mission accomplished. Nonetheless, as the years have passed, a growing interest into my story, life and progress still remains within the 65 million people who my work has reached worldwide. To the thousands who have contacted me over the years, inquiring about who I truly am, this book will answer all of your questions, and much more… within reason.

As many already know, my professional background is founded in psychology. However, my primary occupation is that of a journalist. Nonetheless, it is from my extensive knowledge of these fields, that has afforded myself the qualifications to truly expose Islam for what it is. When I first came to investigate Islam, it would have been around the time America had officially declared 'War on terror', and when G.W. Bush was still trying to find those pesky 'weapons of mass destruction'. Surprisingly, despite over 3000 people dying on 9/11 through the acts of cowardly Muslim terrorists, the media was more interested in the hunt for the arch-boogie man himself, Osama Bin Laden, than actually researching the core tenets of the faith. If anything, a complete white-wash of the religion was already taking place. Nonetheless, it's quite ironic that if 9/11 had not occurred, I most probably would never have embarked on a journey which led to the complete psychological deconstruction of the founder of a 1400 religion. I believe that Islam would have just faded away, and the world would have gone back to spinning. However, this was not the case.

Like most people, Islam was alien to me. From what I had vaguely learned from brief conservations with colleagues was that the faith was similar to Judaism, and also Christianity. But as the years passed, and as terrorism became increasingly attached to our daily life, I decided to passively observe the occasional university lecture or campus debate regarding Muhammad's religion, which were open to the public. It is from that point in time that I would begin to conduct my own personal studies. However, the more I studied, the quicker I was able to learn that the facts absolutely discredited Islam as a religion. As I, and so many had discovered, neither was it a genuine religion, but typically a war-like, disjointed ideology heavily plagiarising Judaism, with a sprinkle of Christianity. What was certainly more evident, was that I was presented with the irremovable truth that Muhammadanism was nothing more than a cult. I still remember the words of the lecturer who so eloquently explained the concept of Islam.

"If Muhammad did it, so must Muslims."

I was really rocked to the core by this simple yet entirely revealing statement, which implied that terrorism, and all the nasty business that comes with Islam was not attributed to a Muslim's personal ambition, but due to one man… Muhammad. This statement in itself, sums up

Islam. From then, I was hooked. For the next 10 years I ate, slept and talked Islam. The more I read of the texts, the more I was shockingly appalled, but still I ventured further into the rabbit hole. While many of my colleagues were enjoying their lives with families, and largely ignoring the rise of Islamisation in the west, I myself dedicated years collating, compiling and analysing virtually every Islamic tradition in accordance with the Quran. Not only in English, but also Arabic. Of course, this was way before the spread of the information superhighway; a term which described the nascent advent of the internet we have access to today.

I poured through the library archives, double-checking every single Hadith verse which described the cult leader in detail. For the layman, the Hadith codex is a vast, sprawling archive, spread out among many different authors. These scriptures are not only the key to understanding Muhammad's mind, but most importantly, the Muslim psyche today. They explain the psychological indoctrination Muslims religiously subject themselves to, the intolerance of non-Muslims, and the desire to kill and die violently for the big lie. And as history dictates, Muslims have not changed in 1400 years. Unlike Christianity and Judaism, the faith has never experienced a reformation, which today still inexorably presents itself as an eccentric, incongruous cult in a modern, progressive society.

As my psychological studies on Muhammad began to envelop my life, I had come to the conclusion that the man was either truly insane, demon-possessed, suffering with a multitude of mental disorders, or perhaps a charlatan. Those who have read my book will know the answer. They will also know that I ruled out the insanity card, as it is through Muhammad's semi-lucid state of mind, where he planned the genocide of thousands through calculated means, which unequivocally

20

proves the man was aware of his actions. This alone proves culpability and rejects the premise of diminished capacity. Instead, I attributed the wealth of psychological disorders to his social circumstances, namely his mother abandoning him at childhood.

While I was already in the final stages of editing my work, I was already witness to the rise of periodic terrorism which increased dramatically since Obama took office. As each attack took place, I felt a strong moral call to duty to expose the religion for its fraudulence. In part, I felt that in some way I could stem the tide by educating Muslims, to deter them from a wasted life of self-abuse and ritual suicide. Of course, it didn't help matters when the liberal media were already downplaying Islamic terrorism as merely a 'hijacked' ideology. And as I slowly saw the west begin to crumble, as it swallowed itself in political correctness, I witnessed first hand how Islam was positioning itself at the head of the table as the arbiter of morality, all aided by the crooked, liberal media, politicians and the U.N.

Something had to be done.

In 2013, I made the documentary called 'The Muslim Agenda', which is a two hour long exposé on the cult, its political teachings and the mandate it maintains to convert the world to Islam, through stealth, or by the sword. It was the best I and my team could do with limited funding, but it effectively gained around a million views through mirroring and unauthorised distribution, where it was featured on various European news websites. It's important to note that our team received absolutely no profit for this venture, which was done out of passion to educate the masses. We could have easily charged people, which would have made us quite wealthy. But this was never our intention.

Because of our hard work, we were proudly mentioned and even promoted by former politician Paul Weston of political party Liberty GB, who used our documentary as a talking point on Facebook to address the rise of Islamization the UK. A year later, Weston was arrested outside a British town hall for reciting Winston Churchill's honest speech on the dangers of Islam. The police were totally unaware that the speech belonged to Churchill, which highlighted their ignorance and betrayal of the father of modern England.

Despite releasing the film, terrorism still was spreading rapidly throughout the west. It was not along after that we saw the Syrian War escalate due to Obama supplying arms and funds to ISIS, which in turn created the migration vacuum to the EU. As the media argued amongst themselves over Islamic politics and middle-east policy, I saw that the solution to end the conflict was not to futilely enter into debate, but to attack the cult directly where the vulnerability lay. As someone with a legal background, it has never been my style to tip-toe around any problem, but to tackle it head on. I knew that by informing the public of the cult's shortcomings, and its teachings, which were undoubtedly dictated by a psychopath, we would have a better chance at defeating Islamic terrorism for good. If Muslims truly understood how demented and fraudulent their beloved prophet was, the eternal Jihad would reach a stalemate.

From the countless hours of seminars, debates, and political discussions I have witnessed, not once did any panelist, journalist or politician ever raise the fact that Muhammad's authorship was the catalyst for the problems we are experiencing today. This disingenuous charade the media played, infuriated me to no end. I knew that if the masses, especially Muslims, were privy to how mentally disturbed Muhammad truly was, no-one would take Islam seriously ever again. It would be banned, declassified from being a religion, and ultimately outlawed.

What was clearly evident, was that the majority of people today, including Muslims, are unable to reconcile Islam and Muhammad. Somehow, Muhammad invariably becomes divorced in the argument, and debates are seldom exercises in comparability of culture, faiths and statistics. However, the Islamic 'system', was allegedly devised by only one man. If the world actually spent more time analysing Muhammad and his example, the Islamic 'system' would indeed unravel, and eventually fall apart. The "religion" itself, or should I say *political cult*, is a house of cards that was built on lies and one man's twisted imagination. I knew that by comparing the Islamic sources with accredited and referenced psychological journals, it would be impossible to disprove that Muhammad was the most psychologically-fractured individual to ever walk the planet.

And so my quest began. After ten years of researching the inner depths of Muhammad's psyche, his habits, behavioural patterns and modus operandi, it was safe to say that I knew the man better than himself. I knew that by only writing a journal to debunk the man's claim to prophethood would not be the most prudent way to bring about change. What was important was the religion itself faced culpability by trial. It is then that I was inspired to write the book as a legal trial to give the people the choice whether to convict or acquit. As Muhammad himself believed that he was superior to Jesus Christ and every major individual named in the Bible, I saw it fitting that the founder of Islam bear responsibility and face trial. Even Jesus Christ faced prosecution, albeit on trumped up charges. Thus, why should Muhammad be any different? Jesus however was innocent, and went quietly to his death, while Muhammad never stood trial, despite his extensive legacy of rape, theft, murder, and obvious spiritual fraudulence.

Until today, 'The People vs Muhammad - Psychological Analysis' is the only book in history to thoroughly dissect Muhammad's personality, and to charge the man with the murder of over 270,000,000 innocent people throughout history. In my book, I make a comparison between every dictator known in the modern age, and still by far, Muhammad was the worst offender to exercise genocide. Alas, it is because of Muhammad that 1.6 billion people on this planet are ready to murder innocent people at the drop of a hat for a narcissistic, homicidal, conceited, pedophile. And that, to me is the primary reason to crush Muhammad, and to bring him to justice.

Writing the book was no easy task. I had to categorise every piece of crucial information into a flowing, intelligible publication that could not be refuted. Apart from the introduction, which outlined the preemptive counter arguments Muslims and liberals use, each chapter was uniquely dedicated to every personality disorder and psychosexual habit I could attribute to Muhammad's bizarre behaviour. As I knew that the book's veracity would be scrutinised to no end, I had disciplined myself to referencing every single piece of information and fact to destroy any refutation. Thus, the book bears over 500 unique references which any Muslim today has not been able to reject.

The ordeal around publishing the book was a whole different matter, and quite an unpleasant experience. After finishing my manuscript, I had sent it to no less than thirty publishers who would have been suitable to benefit from my work. After nearly a year of being stone-walled, left in limbo, and outright rejected, I had come to a roadblock. I recall one major publishing firm telling me with a curt tone, *"There is no way we can publish a book which says that the founder of the most sensitive religion in the world had syphilis! Do you think we're crazy?"* Of course, the conversation abruptly ended when I gave them examples of their hypocrisy, as they had published books which were flagrantly offensive to other religions, namely Christianity.

By the end of the year, I had all but given up. Doubts about my book's future, and my personal efforts were setting in. Suddenly, on one weekday morning, I received a brief email from a publishing company which I had completely forgot about. Their email was positive and very inspiring. After a brief talk, we had decided to list the book under a proxy company name to protect their identity, for obvious reasons. And on June 9th 2015, the first edition of 'The People vs Muhammad - Psychological Analysis' was published.

Since the time of publication in 2015, it has been a very interesting and disturbing path to the present. While it is understandable that new authors seldom receive publicity, my book was not the exception. For some months, it remained in the obscure, dark side of the book retail world. To be frank, the book hardly sold any copies despite its controversial topic and well-timed introduction to the market. I knew that I could not sit back and allow the truth to sit quietly on some shelf while the west was under siege. Thus, I created a campaign to contact as many media outlets as possible to give my book the proper exposure it needed. I recall sending a personal letter to over 150 news stations and Christian organizations. Among these were Fox News' 'Hannity', Alex Jones' Infowars, Breitbart and many more, including countless other Youtube channels supposedly dedicated to combating the Islamization of the west. Regarding 'the church', I also won't mention names, but suffice to say I was truly disgusted and can only warn people to be weary about career 'Christians'. As Jesus said, *"behold I send you out as sheep admidst the wolves."* You shall know them by their fruit.

Not surprisingly, among the aforementioned, not one person contacted me back. To be brutally frank, the support from those who purported to be opponents of Islam were very disappointing. And in some way, I feel betrayed by their silence. I also recall a well-known anti-Islam blogger with a tremendous following, who shall remain anonymous, had the temerity to lie to me when they said that *"I don't promote other people's books, and I never have."* In truth, the blogger had promoted no less than six anti-Islam books. I was appalled that a well-known supposed activist who laid out the alleged "bare naked" facts would go as far as to lie, especially when I had for many years contributed financially to her website because I believed she was legitimate. I was very saddened as I had realised that not all allies are true opponents of Islam, but just agents of opportunity. What was even most disappointing, was that the once beloved Christian organisations I had supported, never had the courtesy to reply. For the minuscule amount that did, they went as far as to imply that my book was divisive, racist and counterproductive; as if truth was an inconvenience. Alas, this was my wake up call to be cautious, and to weed out the genuine from the posers. Nonetheless, after ten years of research and sacrifice, I was still left out in the cold and abandoned by a community who I believed their intentions to be pure.

For the very few personal associates who were aware of my book, their honest words rang true in the face of adversity. For one, their admission that the book was far too hot for the mainstream press to report, was entirely correct. Political correctness had not only infected the liberal left, but also conservative media outlets who also had red lines they would not cross. Perhaps they call it prudence. I call it cowardice.

It seems that those who supposedly oppose Islam in the media, preferred to take the lukewarm approach to tackling the problem, yet never braving the fire. It is from this experience that I learnt that the people whom you've come to admire and respect, are as hollow and disingenuous as they come. In truth, these people are just the elite - those living in the clouds whose feet barely touch the ground. Islam has not affected them in any way. They live comfortable lifestyles and enjoy privileged positions without actually sacrificing anything.

After witnessing the carnage Islam was leaving behind in our countries, and personally seeing neighbourhoods I once lived in turning into Islamic ghettos, I could only say these supposed opponents of the cult were paying us lip service and hollow rhetoric. It was then I knew that I could only rely on myself to seize the day. The following year, I set out to build my own network by reaching out to the common man, and never any media outlet ever again. And in 2016, I founded the online video news network, NBT Zone, which was a Youtube channel dedicated to exposing the rise of Islamization in the west.

The rest is history.

This is how it all went down.

THE TRUTH SETS THE CAPTIVES FREE

As my Youtube channel began to gain immense traction due to the European migration crisis, I simultaneously witnessed my book become a #1 international bestseller. Within weeks, word of my book had reached critical mass and had spread throughout all social media networks like wildfire. Not only did my book top the charts, it was outselling other bestselling authors in many other categories. These authors were Sean Hannity, Glenn Beck, Richard Dawkins, Sam Harris, Christopher Hitchens, Newt Gingrich, Ayaan Hirsi Ali, Robert Spencer and even the Dalai Lama. Sure enough, the reviews started flooding in. The general consensus was overwhelming praise for thinking outside the box, and approaching the problem in a fresh and informative manner. It was hailed by critics and reviewers as not only a "masterpiece", but the most dangerous book ever written, and perhaps the most controversial within the last decade. Of course, these articles were available to read, until Google decided to delete these listings on their search results.

Predictably, it wasn't long before the inevitable tide of online trolls and angry Muslims decided to set up camp on my Amazon listing. Most of the negative feedback was from disgruntled spouses of Muslims, ill-educated simpletons and plenty of flaming liberals. I was accused of attacking Muslims, and being a 'racist', despite the book being solely critical of Muhammad alone. Naturally, I had anticipated the wave of criticism, and had already wrote a preparatory response in my book. Had these fools actually bought and read the book, they would've known this. But this didn't matter to them, as their campaign to undermine went ahead unabated. Fabrications of grammatical errors, spelling and other nonsense was the typical response from a nation of liberal idiots who could not refute the actual facts within the book. As my book was unchallengeable, the liberal hit squad resorted to petty name calling, and accusing my book for using overly 'shouty' and 'big' words, implying that I was overreaching, I suppose. Until this day, I still do not understand what exactly constitutes as a 'shouty' word.

I also recall many of the aforementioned believe they could somehow trap me in what they perceived was a lie written in my book. As I had stated in my book, as 9/11 unfolded I stayed up late at night to watch the events. This confused many people who were unaware that the planet has multiple time zones, especially when I never said I was residing in the USA at the time. Instead of reading the facts and hundreds of references given within the book, they picked on trivial information in attempt to discredit my work. Still, it really didn't make much of an impact as every single 1 star review written during that time did not bear the 'verified purchase' tag. It was clear that most of these fake reviewers were reading only the first few pages within the preview. Despite the ghouls' efforts to take down my book, it was too late… the media had already caught on.

I still fondly remember news commentator and journalist Katie Hopkins, who was fired by LBC Radio for speaking the truth on Islam, give high praise for my work, stating that it was "read with great interest and was very impressed by the level of research committed to the project." It was around this time that LBC had begun to position itself as a Marxist propaganda network, and initiated the great purge of conservative voices. Around four years later, Brexit champion Nigel Farage, a once critical opponent of Islam, joined the radio station, and subsequently changed his critical stance on the cult. Such is the power of intimidation, I can only guess.

Sometime in 2017, around the time when my channel was eventually coming under attack by Youtube's internal goons, I received an email from a publishing clerk within the well-known news and book publishing company, WND News. The case manager wrote to congratulate me on the book's success, stating that I "had done something wonderful." Quite interestingly, I had approached WND to publish my book around two years before, of which they ultimately rejected. In truth, despite the praise and boilerplate congratulations, the clerk ultimately contacted me to find out my secret to success. I accommodated, but in hindsight I should have been frank and said, "Because you missed out on publishing my book, this is the reason why I went it alone… and thus the reason for my success. Thank you."

In retrospect, I didn't need a publishing outfit anyways. With the income I received from the book and Youtube, I was was able to hire a team to research, publish news, edit video, and run continuous publicity campaigns to build on the already immense following. The demand for the book was so overwhelming that it had to be put on priority print at my distributors, which even they were struggling to keep up with demand. For over two years since publication, the book remained consistently on the international bestsellers lists. In Canada, it has stayed at #1 on Amazon's bestsellers for over a year.

As the book continued to sell steadily, our team began to create plans to make a new documentary to warn the masses of the globalists secret plans to Islamize the world. We had spent hundreds of hours pouring through declassified CIA and intelligence intel. From the data we analyzed, we could see a pattern occurring which proved that plans were set to introduce Muslims to every western country to hybridise both our cultures and faiths. Of course, these plans to publish a DVD series went to ruin after our company was censored. Likewise, due to the overwhelming response and pleas from readers to make a feature film for 'The People vs Muhammad', these plans were also scrapped about the same time we applied to run a kickstarter program.

There was no guessing anymore. We were finally under attack.

Around this time, our channel had managed to accumulate over 65 million viewers worldwide, which is proven on my website with multiple documentation. And after fighting every community strike, bogus copyright claim, and whatever the globalist system could throw at us, we still managed to stay online. After three years of publishing, and releasing a new book titled 'Questions that Islam can't answer', we began to receive innumerable emails from former Muslims thanking us for our efforts to bring them away from the cult. This was the big payoff. Not the money, or the notoriety. The real reward was waking people up from a delusion.

However, not long after in late 2018, our channel NBT Zone was shut down and terminated without any strike, violation or reason. The attack came swiftly, calculatingly and diabolically. Until this day, our lawyers have attempted to get a formal response from Youtube's communities department, which have been ignored. We surmise that it was not due to the content, or the fact that the book was outselling most authors on the market, but because Muslims were now turning away from the cult. Officially, we believe that this is the sole reason why why have faced ongoing censorship.

This is how it all happened.

"To learn who rules over you, simply find out who you are not allowed to criticize."

- Voltaire

THE CENSORSHIP BEGINS

Within two years of my book becoming a bestseller, my publishing company had come under fire from Big Tech and political influences. First came the unjustified criticisms, the fake news stories, and of course, the predictable leftist retorts. It's not easy to put oneself out there to the masses, only for an ignorant flock of manipulated liberal fools, who collectively embrace the hatred of their masters, to vent their poison on my life's work. That being said, it still didn't deter me from my cause. However, it wasn't before long that we found out that some of our orders were being smuggled into the Arab states. It was then that things started to *get real*. What followed was a continuous onslaught of death threats. And each day that passed, my email account began to fill with the most extreme, vile, and hateful messages one could expect. The content was so disturbing, that our publisher had no choice but to archive each message, log each I.P address, and take further action. While this was happening, the final step in silencing us came in the form of a total digital takedown offensive.

Despite enjoying relative freedom to express our opinions online, we quickly felt the vice of the liberal technocrats slowly tightening their grip around us. Doors were quickly being closed to us, and the internet was no longer the promised land of opportunity and egalitarianism. We quickly learned that, for a liberal, it's easier to follow the lie than to face the truth. While digital Rome burned, Google, Facebook, Twitter and Youtube all played their own fiddle to the macabre sound of liberty's death rattle. And this all happened while the public was completely unaware what was happening to us. We fought hard to stay online, to preserve our voice, never capitulating or showing weakness in the face of tyranny.

What I didn't realise at the time, was that Islam was, and still is, big business for many in our society. Terrorism creates jobs, allows for the unvetted migration of refugees through orchestrated conflicts, which binds our society tightly with CCTV, counterterrorism bills, and the dreaded 'Patriot Act'. Islam also is the linchpin in the political correctness weapon, whereby the worse acts of violence that Muslims commit, the more the government insists on clamping down on your free speech. This is precisely the reason why my business has been terminated.

Alas, I have stepped on too many toes, and I am now outside the bubble of cultural acceptability. I am too 'hateful', 'bigoted' and 'counterproductive' for the modern laodicean church to embrace. I'm too politically incorrect for the most hardened conservative firebrand, and far too honest for the dishonest media to cover. This era we are facing today is tantamount to a new dark ages, where the elites keep the masses in the dark to fulfil their agenda of totalitarian control over the world. Censorship only proves that the wicked like to hide in the darkness. They will never embrace the truth, for they revel in falsehood, deception, and pure evil to obtain their means.

While there will be many readers who would posit that Big Tech is just a benign conglomerate of private companies, who can terminate anyone's account which they please, the problem is that this 'private' industry has now placed themselves in the firing line for violating antitrust laws. In truth, Big Tech is *the* biggest historical monopoly in the world. The big four are so entwined that there isn't any real competition, as all seem to symbiotically work together in purging people of the conservative persuasion. In layman's terms, they've become too powerful, too quick. And that power equates to one whole entity, which stands against the first amendment. This is textbook antitrust violation.

Regardless of our political views, all citizens have the right to speak freely on these social media platforms, regardless of race, religion, nationality and creed. As American companies, the U.S discrimination code is adamant about these protections, including our first amendment privilege. The term 'Creed' has already been addressed in congress to finalise a permanent protection on citizens', unencumbered speech. Therefore, I cannot understand how Big Tech is getting away with this crime. The U.S government and Attorney General must file antitrust charges against all firms in light of the recent censorship paradigm we are facing. If these companies are opposed to conservatives speaking their mind on social media, then they must allow other competition to fill that demand. This is not rocket science, but a historical fact as we saw Microsoft successfully sued in the late 1990s for antitrust, just for supplying free software.

Censorship today is a whole other issue which flies in the face of the founding fathers and the legacy they fought and bled for. If we do not change the pernicious, Marxist culture spreading through our civilisation, we're already dead. As you will see from the following content, I have broken down a detailed list of the globalist offenders and political thugs who have worked against me to delude the public into a false sense of security. I have taken no liberties with the truth, and I will save the best until last.

FACEBOOK CENSORS ME

The first offender to take away my right to free speech was none other than Facebook. Since the time of my first publication, our Facebook page was gaining steady traction online, and reaching out to tens of thousands a day. Our team was engaging with Muslims, ex-Muslims and all who yearned to learn the truth. Despite the occasional outburst and threat from Islamists, which Facebook always overlooked, we had established good rapport with our community base.

Naturally, it wasn't long before the attempted cyber attacks began. As I have mentioned that our presence online has been shielded through anonymity, this alone infuriated the Muslim community. As such, we received a wealth of phishing emails, deceptive messages, and countless invites to their 'special anti-Islam groups' via fake Facebook profiles which ostensibly appeared to be opponents of Islam, or former Muslims. I might add that despite Facebook's stance on stamping out fake profiles, none of the aforementioned's accounts were terminated. This alone made us deduce that they were created by Facebook's own communities department. It's no secret that an overwhelming amount of Facebook's communities team is based overseas in Muslim dominant countries, or are overseen by Muslim workers back in the states. CEO Mark Zuckerberg could not deny this fact when he had to make a tepid formal apology, stating that his staff were not accustomed to the western mindset, i.e free speech, and that they 'may have made some errors in judgment.' Well, they may have made some illegal errors in silencing people based on their beliefs, but the company made no financial reparations, or reinstatement of their pages.

From the wealth of deceptive phishing communiques we received, the primary motivation was to weed out our geographical location.

Little did these clowns realise that our team is based worldwide, and I never stay in one location long enough due to work commitments. In retrospect, I should have told them I lived in Molenbeek, Brussels, which is the nerve centre of Muslim radicalisation and terrorism. But I digress. Before our termination with Facebook, we ran many promotional campaigns and still were gaining quite a significant presence online. However, we saw the first signs that Facebook had begun its systematic targeting of our page when our post engagement had decreased exponentially by around 70%. On average, our page was at first receiving around 10,000 views per post, and 150 to 200 followers a day, but that quickly changed. During our last days on the platform, we only received around 3 to 5 followers a day, even during the Syrian migration crisis when my book was listed as a bestseller. This alone would baffle any algorithmic mathematician.

As such, we had no choice but to pay for our posts to increase our engagement. At first, Facebook was accomodating to take our money, but we then realised that our posts were going no-where. Despite our campaign informing us that our investment had reached its quota in targeted areas, it appeared that hardly anyone had seen our promotions. To test this anomaly, we ran the campaign again, but this time in areas we knew our targeted audience would definitely see. Again, no-one saw our posts despite the analytics stating they had reached tens of thousands.

But again, this wasn't enough. Facebook then decided to reject all of our paid campaigns on the premise that the content was suddenly 'offensive' and breached their guidelines, despite the images being of the book alone and text. We believe that Facebook's decision to quickly prohibit us from accessing the campaign manager was to cover up their fraudulence and to bury the fact that none of our paid posts were reaching anyone.

At that time, we were also becoming aware that our page follower count was also being throttled. While we were able to manually check to see if the number could increase, of which it did, we could see that it made no difference how many people followed. The number never increased beyond what was obviously being set by the admins. Throughout the months we stayed online, the number remained the same, despite us gaining millions of views on Youtube and other networks. However, we were not the only ones who were being targeted. It seemed that anyone who supported us, or shared our content, was also being silenced. It was clear that the Big Tech methodology was 'guilty by association'. We had a wealth of people contact us stating that their posts relating to my book were being deleted by the admins, and without reason. Without any notice, Facebook was making it publicly known that we were persona-non-grata. And this is how they won, by distracting people with cute animal videos, deleting people off their platform, knowing that the human mind quickly moves on to the next flashing object. In effect, and as a psychologist, I could see that they were employing subliminal, and subtle psychological indoctrination tactics.

But of course, this wasn't enough. In a final move that rendered us obsolete from the network, Facebook suspended our account citing that we engaged in 'spam and misleading practices', and insinuated that our account was created by 'bots'. It was clear that the communities department wanted all traces of our online presence erased entirely. Naturally, we appealed their decision, which was never met with any reply. We were not able to access our data and all communications fell on deaf ears. Predictably, we were sent on a cyclical, wild goose chase through a system of obsolete, broken forms, and defunct email addresses, only to end back where we started. In truth, the whole ordeal felt like a sadistic prank. But this was to be expected as a form of punishment for not conforming to liberal standards. Even more disturbing, was the fact that Facebook had developed a further contact and appeal system which required the customer to upload their government I.D to prove they were who they claimed to be, according to their terms and conditions. This is an invasion of privacy and an outright scam to phish sensitive information from people, no doubt to exploit.

We spoke to our lawyers who advised that what Facebook was doing was completely illegal. No company has the right to ask for a government I.D, especially under such circumstances. The words extortion, coercion and exploitation were also uttered during our legal counsel meeting. Knowing the legal weight Facebook holds, and the insurmountable odds of actually winning, we never bothered to file a suit for discrimination and harassment. Nonetheless, I recall ending our service with Facebook by uploading an image of an "I.D" with the words, "Mark Zuckerberg stole the idea of Facebook, reaped the rewards by having other people build the network, and then scammed his best friend out of his share of the company. Now he is being used as a globalist puppet, and has no soul in his eyes. How's that for 'spam'?"

That was the last time I ever used Facebook. Three years later, Zuckerberg was caught selling customers' data in what could be considered the biggest data breach scandal this decade. I guess it was poetic justice.

It was comforting, but also infuriating to know that we were not the only ones to be terminated for alleged 'spam and misleading content'. Ever since the 2018 America mid-term elections, Facebook removed 559 pages and 251 accounts, in what has been considered a political coup and the biggest purge of conservatives. It is clear that the admins have now resorted to gaming the system for political leverage, of which has introduced us to the arbitrary, fraudulent culture of Silicon Valley where rules don't apply, and decisions are based entirely on personality, mood and tone of voice. But alas, this is the twisted, self-destroying culture they have created which keeps them in bondage. As they feel inherently compelled to destroy more lives, to politically profit, to keep their social status, they eventually ruin the country they live in. The more they please their communist overlords, the more they feel accepted. It's a form of positive reinforcement, and it's become a vicious cycle. And as they've got a taste for it, it won't cease until the core has completed rotted out. The scary fact is that they're taking us down the rabbit hole with them, and there is no escape.

What we found scary, was that our experience with Facebook could be summarised as like dealing with a bunch of petulant frat boys and pre-pubescent morons playing businessman. It would have been nice to actually have dealt with men, and not little boys playing grown-up. The whole setup feels like a secret club, with secret handshakes, and an unspoken code. Of course, these are the hallmarks of an immature subculture, and a nation of latch-key kids. Not surprisingly, there is no staff at Facebook above the age of fifty, and to me that is terrifyingly irresponsible. Imagine an internationally operated conglomerate with billions of dollars in the bank and political influence, hardly pays any taxes, and is being run by a bunch of frat boys, all hardwired with Machiavellian intentions, with no concept of human dignity. This is Facebook. If that prospect doesn't scare you, then nothing will.

But this is the reality of the tech culture today, which is steeped in cultural Marxism. Communistic values are heavily entrenched in Silicon Valley, where they practice the destruction of the middle-class, oppressing the people, revelling in the arbitrary and not the rule of law, rejecting the patriarchy, and denying the existence of God. For it is they who believe that they are now deified. Like Muhammad, who grew drunk on his power, they too have literally lost their minds to delusion. I still maintain and believe that the tech industry has developed some form of obsessive compulsive disorder, whereby they feel compelled to 'clean' the conservative 'filth' off their networks to stay pure to the Marxist faith. Muhammad purged Jews and Christians from the Saudi Arabian peninsular, for "the greater good". Today, the tech overlords are no different.

The irony is that though Mark Zuckerberg is a Jew, he protects Muslims' free speech to threaten, harass and target people on his network, despite Islam calling for the total annihilation of all Jews. Either the man is completely insane, mentally retarded, naive, or all of the above. The man remains a paradox. And that is where the problem lies… he's not a man, which reflects on the platform's ever-puzzling, and risible practices. It speaks volumes for a pathetic, man-child like him to openly ban content which celebrates masculinity and ridicules femininity in men. This is indisputable, when Zuckerberg personally oversaw that the network banned all posts of the 1970s semi-nude photoshoot of deceased actor and the icon of masculinity, Burt Reynolds.

But this is the culture which the west is adopting. Men are no longer allowed to be men, especially on the internet. People like Zuckerberg feel threatened by chest-hair, virility, and the inherent instinct to survive in the wild. This also can't be denied as Facebook banned TV show host Duck Dynasty founder Phil Robertson for simply demonstrating how to prepare a catfish for dinner.

To be honest, I shudder to think what Zuckerberg's childhood was like. Maybe that's the point. He never had one. Perhaps the man is a clone. Who knows? After all, his appearance at the infamous senate inquiry was very telling. Instead of seeing a courageous titan of industry, a man in command of an empire, we were privy to a wispy excuse of a human being. A man-child, with a strange haircut, and even stranger skin tone of greenish-yellow. I don't know about you, but the mere thought of this oddball influencing democracy and the west, is something that keeps me up at night.

While there is literally a plethora of Facebook gaffes and anecdotes which will have you in stitches, in reality, it's no laughing matter. These issues might be trivial at first, but they always metastasise into something more nefarious. Indeed, Zuckerberg is laying the foundations of an evil empire, and we're at the precipice of a communist society.

TWITTER CENSORS ME

Speaking of communists, this brings us to Twitter - the insipid waste of space controlled under the tutelage of liberal hipster, dictator and soy boy Jack Dorsey. In truth, I regard this firm as the 'Johnny come lately' of the big four social tech giants. Historically, the social media platform is seldom the first to take major steps to silence conservatives, but it's a sure bet that they will eventually when other platforms step up to the plate. Like Facebook and Google, Twitter is also run by adolescent nitwits with underdeveloped brains who adhere to political influences that continue to undermine conservative growth, while determining what content should be public according to their rapidly fluctuating hormone levels. Half the people who work there are no doubt on some kind of hormonal replacement therapy, due to the increase of transgenders working in Silicon Valley. I guess it's no surprise why many conservatives have been booted off the platform for no reason, when the network is being monitored by emotionally damaged victims of liberalism.

By far, Twitter is the most indirect form of censorship we have faced, but they have certainly proven that we are on Silicon Valley's black list. The methodology is very simple. Before my Youtube channel was terminated, we had amassed millions of viewers. Analytical data proves that viewership steadily increased from the low millions in 2016, up to around 65 million or more in late 2017. Despite being exposed to literally millions of people world-wide for over two years, and with our channel booming, our Twitter account barely reached more than 700 followers. If we are to mathematically break this down, on average around 2-5% of viewers will seek out a Twitter profile to follow. By taking the figure of 65 million and working with that conversion rate, our Twitter account should have at least gained around 1 million followers or more. Undeniably, what we can see is that our account has been throttled through manual manipulation. There is simply no other logical explanation for why we have such a meagre following. At present, the account has roughly around 8500 or more posts. Any user of the platform would agree that the numbers simply do not add up.

In 2017, we began to use the services of Buffer.com, which is a queue-based, automation service which large brand names use to inform their followers. Our posts were based on an hourly basis, providing unique promotional content, and shared news stories. While engagement was tepid to say the least, within months we noticed that the analytics proved that even these posts failed to engage. We contacted a number of independent social media analysts and experts, all who could not offer a tangible reason why our account was remaining in the dark. Most, if not all, agreed that it was not an algorithm error, but simply malicious intervention. Our account was not allowed to grow organically, and it was obvious that liberal interference was the answer. One of the analysts out right said it correctly, "You're being shadow-banned. They just want you gone."

Shadow-banning is Twitter's trump card. Even if you follow their rules, play nice, but share an alternative viewpoint from liberalism, they resort to turning your volume down. For months, we believed that our posts were being published on all included hashtags, but after inspecting them in *private* or *incognito mode*, they never showed up. Shadow-banning works by giving the account holder the false perception that their posts are being published on all hashtags, when in reality only the poster can see their content, and no-one else. Twitter consistently resorted to this method whenever a terrorist attack occurred, which only proves that 'trends' today are simply manipulated by Silicon Valley. Nothing is organic. It's all fake, and orchestrated. The less the public is aware, or engages in a topic, the trend will move to the next issue. We have also discovered that if any other user is to post to the hashtags, #jksheindlin, #peoplevsmuhammad or include my domain name, they too invariably are placed under a shadow ban. I'm not joking. This is how serious the globalists treat my presence online.

In regards to my follower count being throttled, there is another anomaly which is quite disturbing. Anytime I uploaded a crucial video, post, or anything at all, my follower count would, and will suspiciously drop dramatically. This is typical of Twitter's style of psychological negative reinforcement. We know this isn't paranoia, as the evidence is quite axiomatic. If anything, post creation which is compatible with followers' interests, will most likely gain more followers, not lose them. Instead, within hours, we would see our follower count plummet inexplicably. This even occurred when we stopped sharing content, which is also illogical. The reason being is that a user would need to search for our profile, among the hundreds they follow, then remove us from their list. For anyone to go out of their way to do so, would be intangible. Even today, our follower count never did, or has exceeded what Twitter has limited us to. This is not fantasy but the dangerous reality of the rigged system of social engineering - reward the obsequious quislings, and throttle the non-compliant until they cede. I have already been contacted numerous times by followers who have asked me directly why they were no longer on my follower list. The proof is in the pudding.

While I no longer use Twitter at all, I will keep the account open as public proof. If they terminate my account to cover up the truth, I win. If they keep it active, proving how they've throttled my growth, I also win. What is definitely obvious, is that the company is following the liberal policy of gaslighting victims to make them feel as if they're going crazy. This is a common tactic with communists who use mind-control games to get the masses in order. Anyone who speaks out against the insidious manipulation and social engineering, is called a 'conspiracy theorist'. But like they say, *there is no smoke without fire.*

In reality, Twitter is indeed the most insidious and cunning platform to silence opponents of the establishment. While other social media networks simply ban people, or terminate their account, as we can see, Twitter's approach is more diabolical and pragmatic. They know that publicity always surrounds people who are banned or censored. This empowers the victim, and creates a counter-effect which drives more traffic to their cause. Twitter does not want this, and will tarry until the bitter end before terminating an account; and this usually happens only when the other tech giants have set the precedent.

Shadow-banning and throttling is a devious form of censorship, and no doubt the brainchild of a Machiavellian psychologist which Twitter keeps on the payroll. For only a psychopath or trained expert in psych war could cook up this technique. Psych war experts know that the human mind is wired to quickly forget confronting issues when the attention dies down. By giving the impression that the 'trend' is ending, people move on to the next topic. This is how propaganda quickly turns a nation against itself, or on others. Twitter's anti-constitutional, anti-American tactics are truly unethical and disgraceful. To be blunt, we are living in a revived cold-war era, where political enemies such as myself are snuffed out with Stasi-esque tactics. And I'm not alone on this issue. There are literally thousands of unpublished cases of patriots who have been placed in Silicon Valley's trash can. Their crime? Speaking the truth.

To be be honest, we must recognise the real reason why my account has been nobbled, as it's no surprise that Twitter was majority owned by the brutal Islamic Saudi regime. This alone is a conflict of interest, some might say. But let us bypass political correctness, and just speak the truth, in that Twitter is indeed a state-sponsored puppet, whose oil-influenced partnership promotes global censorship and social engineering.

GOOGLE CENSORS ME

The birth child of globalist puppets Larry Page, and alleged Soviet refugee Sergei Brin, Google is the ultimate monolith that will spell the end of western civilisation, unless it is stopped. Brin's parents would die of shame if they understood what he is doing. That is of course, if they were truly Soviet escapees, or were planted in America by the Kremlin. Who would know for sure? But what we all can agree on, is that Google today has become synonymous with world domination and tactics used by the former Soviet empire to control citizens. This draconian, dictatorial corporation insidiously hides behind their ubiquitous, brightly coloured logo, but in reality, it's the most pernicious, sinister force this side of history. While Google might own Youtube, and control its directives, I have saved my experience with that platform until last for reasons you will later understand.

In regards to this particular monolith, both Google and Facebook share an incestuous relationship, where each was handpicked by the NSA to reap your data. They did this quietly for many years before being caught with their pants around their ankles. But in recent days, the money and power lies in deciding who gets to speak, and who remains in the shadows. Elections are won or lost on free speech and public influence, and this scares the tech elite to no end. In truth, Google is no longer a private corporation out to make money. Quite the contrary, they've made their fortune, and have transcended into the largest political organisation which is irremovably steeped in Marxist ideological principles. Former Google employee, James Damore, knew all too well how pernicious the company is, when he was fired for standing up against their discriminatory practices of not hiring white and asian people. It seems that the issue of 'diversity' is the latest weapon of 'divide and conquer', which is binding the Marxist hive together in Silicon Valley. It has nothing to do with race, but to weed out those who are not on board with their biased practices. What they say goes. Any if anyone resists, they must be destroyed.

This is what the corporation has become. It's no longer a source for knowledge, but a curated information think-tank designed to change and influence western culture, swing elections, dull the masses, and to control how you think. And in a climate where the unfettered truth about Muhammad is a liability to the establishment, it was only a matter of time until I became persona-non-grata on Google. To be frank, Google's censorship of our company wasn't as conspicuous as Facebook in the beginning, but it became quite disturbing nonetheless by 2017. From what we can see, the corporation's tactic was through systematic replacement, and subtle conditioning. Of course, this is typical of a state-sponsored intelligence puppet, where new experimental politics are always introduced very slowly to avoid detection. Google played their part well, and by the start of 2017, had successfully managed to bury every single positive article and news story written about my book. This was not an algorithmic error. On the contrary, our Youtube channel was booming, as viewers were adding up into the tens of millions. It was because of Google's symbiotic relationship with Youtube which was the reason why my book suddenly was being slowly erased off the largest, most powerful search engine in history. The company was keeping their most detrimental move against me until last. This being, the takedown of my channel.

Even today, Google has removed the majority of all positive information about my books from their search listings. There used to be a wealth of articles written by independent journalists, blog sites and former Muslims. Today, any search into my name, or the book, returns a perfunctory result with a negative tone. More disturbingly, my website is barely mentioned or categorised in its entirety in the search listings. If you were not careful, you could miss it among the other distracting, and contrived listings showing slanderous, defamatory fake news websites.

As the months went by in 2017, we could see that our online presence was quickly shrinking. It was clear that I had been placed on the eternal black list as any article that was written to introduce my book to the public, was wiped clean from Google's listings within weeks. Adding to the frustration, I had also experienced a lot of my emails disappearing or being sent to people's junk mail. Of course, it was our mistake to use Gmail, but we would never have thought that Google would go as far as to manipulate our communications.

In 2018, a leaked document which originated from Google's most inner sanctum was publicly exposed, which was called 'The Good Censor'. The 85 page document is truly an eye-opener, and as we read it thoroughly, our hearts sank. It was clear that I was certainly the 'canary in the coal mine', as the document highlighted almost every single tactic Google has used in undermining my publishing business. The document has since become known as the Google bible, and is the cornerstone of the company's policy when dealing with conservative content. In brief, the document encourages employees to manually manipulate data by gaming algorithms, and to clamp down on content which is in conflict with liberal principles. Not only is content a threat, but the overlords in Google believe that policing 'tone of voice' is in fact more important. As you will see later on in this book in regards to my Youtube account, I highlight how I was one of the first victims to be persecuted under this new draconian rule. Likewise, in later chapters, I give a detailed blow by blow of 'The Good Censor', which I'm sure you'll find shocking.

Like Facebook, Google is another company which flagrantly evades taxation through Cayman Island offshore accounts. It is through this virtually illegal tax loop-hole which has allowed the corporation to metastasise and become the cancerous, un-American den of vipers it is today. There is no secret why Google's content policing policies have ramped up since the corporation hired CEO Sundar Pichai - a spindly, rat-faced man who has quickly forgotten the oath he took to defend the constitution, especially the 1st amendment, during his confirmation of American citizenship. As the oath states…

> "I hereby declare, **on oath**, that I absolutely and entirely renounce and abjure all allegiance and fidelity to any foreign prince, potentate, state, or sovereignty, of whom or which I have heretofore been a subject or citizen; that **I will support and defend the Constitution** and laws of the United States of America against all enemies, foreign and domestic; that I will bear true faith and allegiance to the same; that I will bear arms on behalf of the United States when required by the law; that I will perform noncombatant service in the Armed Forces of the United States when required by the law; that I will perform work of national importance under civilian direction when required by the law; and that I take this obligation freely, without any mental reservation or purpose of evasion; **so help me God.**"

Which god does Pichai serve? Certainly not the God of the Bible who gives us free will and speech to choose. Perhaps Pichai was given a different oath, omitting these crucial tenets. If Pichai ever swore allegiance to the flag, I suppose the concept of "with liberty and justice for all" would be alien to a man who lives above the law and disrespects the republic's freedoms for which they stand. Is the man even familiar with the concept of liberty? Evidently not. Perhaps his immigration lawyer expedited his citizenship papers, while failing to inform his client that America is the land of the free, not a landscape for looting and pillaging the populous from their God given rights. It seems that this pseudo-American still has his roots entrenched in Indian culture, where his home country is still in the grasp of a caste system which does not view equality as a virtue. It seems that Pichai has again violated his oath in this regard, as all new citizens must renounce any allegiance to foreign influences, including ideologies such as the caste system. Consequently, it is Pichai's oriental and pagan influence which has seen the steady demise in free speech on the platform.

Pichai has for the longest time been suspected of being a closet Muslim, a fact which the tech industry hides knowing how the American public would not tolerate foreign ideological infiltration, and the fact that America's former president ran the country into the ground due to his faith. It's no secret that the 'ghost president' Barack Obama is undoubtedly a closet homosexual Muslim, and we all know how that influenced America. For eight years, the USA became a hotbed of terrorism, and we witnessed the president make every excuse possible for Islam's obvious terroristic tenets, while he boldly projected the rainbow 'gay pride' flag on the White House to embolden the militant LBGTI movement - a proxy Marxist organisation whose only goal is to seize power, not spread equality.

These are Google's core principles today, and it's all due to Obama. In truth, both shared an incestuous relationship and a common goal to destroy America from within. It is because of Obama that homosexuality and transgenderism today is the ultimate political power card, which compels speech, emboldens censorship, and punishes those who are apolitical or wish to remain silent. Through Big Tech's persistent brainwashing via their platforms, conservatives are now labelled by default as instigators and hate-mongers due to the Bible's teachings on homosexuality. The liberal elites have played this to a tee, and it's all due to Obama; a man who married a transgender, from developing a sexual attraction to the phenomena through his time raised by a tranny in Indonesia, and especially after being born in Kenya - a fact that his home country is proud of where they display the sign *'Welcome to Kenya. Birthplace of Barack Obama'*. It's also no surprise that Kenya just so happens to have a history entrenched in Communism and Soviet ideals.

There's no secret that the man was caught through forensic analysis to have falsified his birth certificate, in the event that investigators would discover that his mother was not actually a US citizen. What is certain, is that she was a Soviet born spy who married a Marxist community organiser, whom ran a hardcore pornography racket for the communists to blackmail assets. It just so happens that Obama's father used his wife as an actress for such films. This is documented widely, but also buried in the internet. If anyone is to study Obama's family history, documents show that both his parents admit to having met at a Russian language class. It is my opinion that they most likely fabricated their 'American roots', just like their son did come election time.

One must ask themselves, why did Obama feel the need to forge a phoney birth certificate, pretending to be born in Hawaii? After all, being born in Kenya would not disqualify him from the presidential race, as his mother allegedly was an American citizen. In fact this would have worked to the Democrats favour, as a Kenyan born, *black* president would be a boon for their political agenda. The simple answer is that his mother wasn't American. End of story.

Another important question is why would Obama's mother need to invest her time in a taboo language, especially when American companies were shunning communists throughout the cold war? Russian was certainly not in vogue at that era, and would have been more of a liability than an asset. Very simply, Obama's mother was a CIA turned asset, or double agent, of which this fact is quickly gaining publicity. She was most certainly assigned to Russian language schools and the community to recruit interested parties to the Marxist cause, whereby she met her Kenyan, communist husband. Thus the enigma lies in intelligence recruitment. In truth, the public are already deducing that Obama was a CIA plant, whose mandate was to embolden Big Tech. The entire Obama family is steeped in the deep state intelligence community, and more so, in communist values. This explains why the ideology of the 'evil empire' rubbed off so well on ol' Barry.

CIA and NSA are responsible for the rise of Google, which also explains why outside influences, such as Communist China, are controlling the company. It also demonstrates that Obama's communist legacy for censorship through Big Tech, his parents' sordid past, and the Marxist values spreading from Silicon Valley is the reason why we must rigorously vet and scrutinise our future leaders. Like Obama, if the foreign born Pichai continues to run Google the way Stalin ran Russia, it would make Obama's administration look like romper room. Google is set to become the premier internationalist, state-run corporation to control your life. It already has incorporated G-Pay in most payment systems worldwide, and has seized the role of universal morality arbiter and biased information curator. It is undoubtable that Google will financially block customers from using their payment system who possess 'hateful' social media content. The company is already in violation of antitrust, of which it was fined for in the EU, but this isn't enough to stop it, and the world governments know this. If Google seizes the financial payment industry, much the same way gateway processor PayPal has dominated online payments for over twenty years, how long do you think you will last if Google does indeed seize political power to control the world?

YOUTUBE CENSORS ME

In regards to the censorship throughout the social media landscape, I have left the worst until last. By far, the most ruthless of the big four, Youtube has imposed numerous Anti-American, draconian rules on its community which has garnered immense negative feedback from creators. The Youtube of today pales in comparison to the Youtube of yesterday. It has become an over-commercialised, poppy, ADHD riddled, whitewashed community, full of millennial quislings, which somehow still bears a fringe element of a dying rebellion.

Youtube stars who have been granted the ultimate privilege to grow their channel into the tens of millions, are oddly similar to each other. In most cases, the most popular Youtubers are nothing but braindead millennials, peddling their wares, liberal beliefs, to beguile an impressionable gullible audience. These unsuspecting stooges are merely puppets for the globalist agenda. For these liberal fools who have sold their souls and crawled on their knees while cap in hand to appease their overlords, they are nothing more than the walking dead - white sepulchres who are rotting on the inside, while pretentiously feigning purity and futile compliance. Indeed, Youtube has become a soulless platform devoid of its former grit. It is because of the zombie-like attitudes of the liberal conformists, who are completely sapped of individuality and expression, is why I now call the network 'Ghoultube'.

By far, Youtube will go down in history as the most pernicious brainwashing tool the establishment has ever devised. And it can't be denied as statistics report that over five billion videos are watched on the platform everyday. The power the network holds to subliminally brainwash the masses is truly confronting. Moreover when the tech oligarchs of today are no longer concealing their intentions to divide the west by placing conservatives, Christians, and the alt-right into the minority. The digital apartheid is no longer some ideal that was harboured in the back of liberal minds. Today, it is Silicone Valley's policy. All who fail to conform must sit at the back of the bus, and walk in the gutter to make way for the tech elitists.

Less than three years ago, you could somewhat rely on Youtube to honestly curate your video feed with either popular or fledgling videos with actual content that was erudite. Now, a user must dedicate their time to conscientiously find compelling, honest videos, which is usually an exercise in futility. Simply put, it's almost impossible to find content which hasn't been slanted by liberals. It's evident that 'anything' which scares the leftist folk must now be buried deep within the system, or completely taken down. I challenge the reader to search for any video on the platform which portrays Islam negatively. Go ahead, type the word 'Islam' and you'll be met with saccharine, overly ingratiating and flattering videos which praise Muhammad, the faith and the ecumenical movement.

The era of religious criticism, spearheaded by Dawkins, Hitchens, Hirsi Ali and more, has gone the way of the dodo. Simply put, Muslims are now a protected class, which shockingly was actually acknowledged in verbatim by Facebook CEO Mark Zuckerberg. While Facebook certainly has gone on a censorship binge, Youtube is undoubtedly the mother of all political purge mechanisms. The Youtube we have today might be under the control of CEO Susan Wojcicki, but in reality the platform is undoubtedly the brainchild of Sundar Pichai; a man who is paid around $200 million a year to profit from the misery of society. There is no doubting that since Pichai took control of the company in 2015, coincidentally the same year my first book was published, Youtube's algorithms have been noticeably amended to directly attack and suppress conservatives, truthers, libertarians, while equally preventing the public from receiving anything negative about Islam.

It's also disturbing that as my channel was terminated without good reason or notice, the ghouls in the high tower have not only allowed pedophiles to keep their channels, but to continue profiting from them through ad revenue. I'm not joking. In September 2018, channel owner Ian Rylett of 'SevenSuperGirls' was arrested for molesting a child in a hotel, yet it took Youtube nearly a year to remove his channel. Of course, this was due to Rylett being a money maker for the platform. Likewise, Youtube and also Facebook banned video vigilante Zach Sweers, know as 'Anxiety War', who posed as a minor to trap pedophile predators. But Sweers is not alone. For years, Kyle 'Dudecomedy' from channel 'MrTechnicalDifficult', was ruthlessly targeted by Youtube's communities department for luring out pedophiles while streaming video from the Chat Roulette platform.

Five years ago, content creators were afforded the privilege to support their families by making a full-time career out of Youtube through such virtuous deeds. Today, they've all given up on the platform due to restrictions, and through aggressive ostracisation. Suffice to say, there are many others who have been ruined by Youtube's communities department, which is undoubtedly a network of creepers who protect their own and unashamedly celebrate pedophilia. One may think that these are isolated cases, but in fact it is now Youtube's standard policy for online conduct and content to punish the virtuous. Evidently, Youtube believes it's totally acceptable to wipe out an entire channel which is spreading the truth, but at the same time, finds it horrifically abhorrent to punish pedophiles who use the platform to groom little children. The irony is that liberals and social justice warriors are quick to pounce on free speech advocates, but tip toe around serious issues such as child rape. And it is from these double standards as to why I also have been terminated from the network.

What Youtube tried to conceal is that my book has indeed reached millions of people worldwide, a fact that Muslims ostensibly ridicule, but know that it is the truth. Our channel NBT Zone was the largest anti-Islam channel on the network which contained around 276 unique videos, all relevant to the rise of Islamization in the west. We had amassed around 100k subscribers, which was quite a feat since that we didn't rely on affiliates. If you were to type the word 'Islam' in Youtube's search bar, without a doubt our videos were always listed on the first page, and then some. It is because of this, and the fact that Youtube could not alter the algorithm lest they be caught out, is why our channel was quickly terminated. Another reason was that my books were being mass-promoted through **65 million viewers world-wide**. While Youtube tried to conceal this by shutting us down, we took the precaution to screenshot every piece of evidence months before the termination. However, the actual viewership number is actually higher than reported. In fact, Socialblade.com shows a flaw in Youtube's calculations, and accurately states that I had reached around **71 million viewers**. All of this documentation is supported on my website. But let's look at the bigger picture. 71 million viewers is approximately the population of the UK, or around three times that of Australia. This is the reason why we were targeted.

Our eventual termination was not due to obscene or graphic content. On the contrary, we were careful not to overtly step over the line. Most, if not all, were pertinent videos on debates, news features, and statistics. With each video we posted, they contained a small promotional slot at the end of the clip, which informed people about my first book. This practice has been accepted by Youtube for as along as I can remember, as many other famous liberal Youtuber's have built their career on promoting their wares in an identical fashion. No other channel has been terminated for spam or misleading conduct as we were, because this practice is completely in accordance with the community guidelines. It's important to mention that not once did we ever flood the network with repetitive and identical content, which is the definition of spam. Besides, why would we do so, considering the wealth of new content to be uploaded each day?

As we've learned over the years, Google does not ban conservatives because of content, but will terminate your account due to your growing popularity. In truth, popularity scares the elites to no end. They know that grassroots programs and political movements can spread like wild fire. This explains why there is still one name which has Capitol Hill's underpants in a twist, and the corrupt flying out of the country. It's a name that represents the will of the people, and their desire to clean up corruption and take back our sovereignty.

That name is 'Trump'.

It might be just a name, but this is how the corrupt fall. The tech elites know that regime changes always start with one person, which is the reason why there are other libertarians such as myself who have faced the wrath of Silicon Valley. Our crimes was not for inciting the rabble, but for inspiring the people. It is evident now that Youtube has recognised the power the platform wields in allowing true and positive change for the better. I am sure that they never anticipated their own network would be the catalyst for righteous societal change and to overthrow their own corrupt, liberal agenda. Such is the danger of wielding a double edged sword.

Despite Trump sailing into office on the populist vote, there is still something quite elusive about the man. What is most striking, is that despite the tough talk to 'drain the swamp' and to protect the people's voice, nothing really has been done about online censorship. Sure, there's been a couple of senate hearings, meetings at the White House, but nothing has changed drastically to undo the bias. So, if anyone was to ask me today about my feelings about the man, I would have to say that I am seriously disappointed, and wholly are starting to believe that he may indeed be controlled opposition. Time will tell.

That being said, it might be an open secret now that Silicon Valley has begun its agenda to stifle free speech, it was indeed planned years ago. As we can see in the leaked Google memo 'The Good Censor', it makes the bold statement on p66-68 and 70 that the company is indeed committed to "shifting towards censorship." But even months before this memo was written, an unknown user on the free speech site 4chan.org made a shocking revelation about the security of our private information, and Silicon Valley's mandate to actually ruin lives.

The following leaked memo is a terrifying look at Google's unbridled and relentless thirst for power through their internal flagging team. As you will learn, there certainly is an agenda, a careful plan of action, and it is all achieved by spying on your browser cookies. However, don't complain. It's our fault for never reading the fine print on the cookies notification. Here is what the developer had to say…

"I'm a developer at Youtube and I've come here to warn you all about something the development team was ordered to do from the higher ups at the company. Currently, internet users are 'flagged' in the system based on Google and Youtube search histories and websites visited. We compile data and user information about which sites are visited most frequently and come up with a 'personality profile' we have set categories up for. One of these categories is listed as "high risk" which are usually internet users who frequent conservative message boards and websites, view Youtube videos we also monitor, and other such areas of the the internet.

Right now, 4chan users are heavily monitored, particularly those of you who request /pol/. **We collect a lot of data about you, including where you live, where you work, and many other things you'd be pretty shocked to know about.** We compile this data and share it with certain government groups and independent think thanks such as the Southern Poverty Law Center. The CIA, NSA, and FBI collect vast amounts of this data as well. Now, while this shouldn't really come as a surprise to you, I think that you may want to take heed of is that **Google is sharing some of this information with leftist groups whose goals are to destroy the lives of these people who fall under the these conservative groups.** These groups are 'unseen' for the most part, and go under pseudonyms to conceal the identity."

- Unknown profile, 2/21/18 Wed, 22:12pm

While this was an anonymous post, we did our homework, and the information indeed checked out. It was certainly verifiable. This only proves that my channel's sudden and unjustified takedown was not a conspiracy theory, but was an orchestrated attack by a legion of demonic ghouls, all employed by Google. But as history shows, since the birth of my channel NBT Zone, Youtube tried many times, albeit unsuccessfully, to close my channel. Unfortunately for them, their community guidelines were still in their nascent stage, and were not exercised to their full capabilities until the ink was dried.

What first started with subtle manipulations such as changing my video thumbnails, forcing us to change the title text, proceeded to a more heavy-handed and conspicuous approach. Naturally it would take a 'flagging army' to bring my channel down, and by ignoring Youtube's own guidelines to achieve their goal. Like a true liberal, they had to play dirty. Thus, it is no surprise that Google finally admitted it works with the Southern Poverty Law Centre to flag content which conflict with liberal thought. But as the above leaked memo states, their relationship was actually formed years before. Equally so, what was kept secret is that the SPLC mandates that 'conservatives' were to be classified as "hate groups", akin to terrorists.

> "We work with over 100 organizations as part of our Trusted Flagger program and we value the expertise these organizations bring to flagging content for review. All trusted flaggers attend a YouTube training to learn about our policies and enforcement processes."
> - YouTube spokesperson - reported on the Daily Caller

The double standards through Silicon Valley is certainly disturbing. For example, in Google's leaked memo 'The Good Censor', it warns about harassment, yet on page 54 it approves of a 27,000 strong left-wing social media army, referred to as a 'digital flash mob' which engages in counter activity; or in other words cyber harassment and bullying. Again, this alone explains why my channel was terminated, and substantiates 4chan's anonymous developer's leaked post.

The first of my videos to face the wrath of the online thugs, were my promotional book trailers. For anyone who has seen these promotional videos, the footage was merely a montage of various terrorist events, but it also demonstrated everyday Muslim aggression and self-abuse. Not surprisingly, they were deemed 'offensive and graphic' by the soy boys up in San Jose. But this is to be expected as liberal snowflakes have been conditioned to silence all criticism of Islamic violence, but ironically are quick to call ANTIFA to assault innocent people. But I'm digressing. As the months went by, there were plenty of other videos of mine which were taken down too. But this is where the tech elites really started to flex their muscles. While we were certainly careful not to upload 'graphically offensive material', this ultimately didn't matter. The attacks came quickly, calculatingly, and ruthlessly.

Evidently, our content merely did not fit the liberal narrative. To test the boundaries of Youtube's capricious communities, I created a mini-documentary showing how bad the situation had become during the height of the Syrian migration crisis in the EU. The video was factually titled, "Migrants bring flesh eating virus to the EU." Analytical data shows that the video reached around 1 million views, which we were quite proud of. However, within a month the video was systematically stripped of a number of privileges. It wasn't taken down, or banned, but received something no-one has ever seen before. This entailed Youtube disabling the comments section, the like and rating button, the subscription button, and most importantly, the share button. Finally, only people aged above 18+ and with a Youtube account were allowed to see it. The video itself was eerily isolated from the network, but still was somehow allowed to be played. All relevant videos on the right side of the screen were blurred out and inaccessible. It was truly bizarre. To be honest, the whole ordeal was identical to how the Soviets would knock down a suspected dissident's front door, and remove their furniture, bedding and food as punishment. While many would consider Youtube's actions to be childish, I believe them to be nefarious and underhanded.

One may ask, why didn't Youtube just take the video down?

Well, the problem was that the video was entirely truthful, yet so shocking that they didn't know what to do with it. They couldn't ban it, as it didn't cross the line. After all, it was just a montage of various news clips, nothing graphic, just the raw facts. Facts that informed the viewer about the Muslim rape crisis, migrant diseases, the Christmas market attack, the EU government secretly ferrying Muslims in at night, and former President Angela Merkel's intention to bring a further 15 million Muslims to the EU and visa free travel for Turkish residents. No doubt, many will believe that it was probably the 'tone' of my video which perturbed the ghouls in the high tower. After all, Youtube is a happy place where people have to go around with smiles plastered on their faces, like a cult. Thus is the power of delusion. But in truth, it was the raw facts which were scaring the ghouls in Silicon Valley. Nonetheless, in November 2018, we received an email from Youtube stating that the video was now effectively blocked in the following countries:

"Austria, Belgium, Bulgaria, Switzerland, Cyprus, Czechia, Germany, Denmark, Estonia, Spain, Finland, France, United Kingdom, French Guiana, Guadeloupe, Greece, Croatia, Hungary, Ireland, Israel, Italy, Lithuania, Luxembourg, Latvia, Martinique, Malta, New Caledonia, Netherlands, French Polynesia, Poland, Saint Pierre and Miquelon, Portugal, Reunion, Romania, Sweden, Slovenia, Slovakia, French Southern Territories, Wallis and Futuna, Mayotte."

What was certainly puzzling, was that the channel was already suspended in late September. Perhaps it was an automated algorithm attack. Who knows?

Likewise, another 'scary' video I uploaded which faced the chop was, 'London and the great white flight.' However, this video was merely a re-upload of a BBC news story. But because I uploaded it, even with the exact same title, Youtube decided to terminate it on the grounds that it was offensive. I appealed unsuccessfully and told the ghouls to vent their frustration on the left-wing BBC if they had problems with the content. After all, I didn't create it. Nonetheless, my appeal fell on deaf ears. Most disturbingly, the video was available to watch on other people's channels, with the exact same title. It was clear that Youtube was singling me out personally.

There were countless other videos on my channel which were taken down for idiotic reasons. One video takedown which really had me shaking my head was a news story about the video game 'Pokemon Go' being banned in the Arab states for idolatry. There was no conservative slant, nothing derogatory said. Just the facts laid bare. Youtube's reason for the take down? "Spam and misleading content." This underhanded, passive-aggressive form of bullying continued for years. Always anticipating another video to be taken down, we truly felt like we were engaged in a sadistic game of hopscotch, but instead stepping on landmines. I can't tell you how disturbing it was to log in to see that another video was flagged and removed, for pathetic reasons given. We would be met with the full red screen message forcing us to comply with their ever changing liberal values, and with each takedown notice, came the dreaded three month probationary time. Youtube gives all channels a three strike policy, and with each strike, your channel functions are slowly stripped away, including uploading. In 2016, I recall that we were down to our last strike, which wasn't the first time. There was no guessing that Youtube was indeed toying with us. As soon as one strike was removed, they would flag another video, putting us on notice once again. In truth, we were being intimidated and harassed. There was really no rules we could follow to please the people in the high tower. We were on their permanent shit list, and there was nothing more we could do.

With Youtube's aggressive community strike policy, the company truly has the online community cornered. Try uploading any conservative video and keep within the rules, and I promise you that the liberal ghouls will still terminate your account based on the broad definition of each guideline created. There is no escape. I call these 'The Liberal Red Lines', as they replicate the draconian rules enforced around the Arab states, North Korea and China. The term 'Red lines' was actually coined during the 1979 Iranian revolution. Today, we are experiencing the exact same censorship which that nation has endured for over thirty-nine years.

Here are the community guidelines which have been propagated throughout all social media networks. As you will now learn, these rules only apply to conservatives, not liberals.

SPAM AND MISLEADING CONTENT

The definition of spam was once quite simple; repetitive and identical content such as 'copy and paste' messages. Today, the term is applied to content which is propagating fast and does not conform to the liberal narrative. Spam is the liberal's version of 'negative trending.' Whether it be reporting on Muslim rape gangs, or the EU's secret migration pact deal to import 54 million Africans, it's still spam. According to Youtube, if the story is gaining traction, it must be fake and misleading, on the premise that only Youtube manually sets the trends. This alone proves that the system is rigged. On a more disturbing note, the actual icon on their policies page concerning 'Spam and misleading content' is a grinning thief. So really, they're implying that I'm a dishonest person, which is quite libellous and defamatory. The word 'scam' is also mentioned in the text. Therefore, my book must be considered as a scam because in the eyes of a liberal, Muhammad is a perfect man.

BULLYING

Bullying is unacceptable. We get it. But when it comes to liberals harassing, stalking, intimidating and maligning libertarians, it's perfectly acceptable according to Youtube. Not once have I ever seen a liberal channel removed for inciting hatred against a certain conservative, or for uploading a left-wing slanted clip sympathising with the actions of the terrorist group ANTIFA. You can do your own searches and see the wealth of bullying videos which Youtube has kept online. This guideline alone represents probably the biggest double standard on the platform. It's evident today that critical news stories, which call out the corrupt liberal establishment, are considered as bullying. After all, we can't hurt the feelings of the ghouls who are ruining lives. This guideline was infamously enforced on Alex Jones for criticising one-minute wonder David Hogg, whose short lived rants over gun-control were panned and ridiculed by all conservatives. Of course, Pichai quickly saw to it that Jones became the fall guy for 'bullying a child.'

VIOLENT AND GRAPHIC CONTENT OR HARASSMENT AND CYBERBULLYING

According to Youtube, it's perfectly acceptable for a left-wing channel to upload a live execution from Saudi Arabia, but when I do it, it's considered 'violent and graphic'. But it doesn't end there. The recent trend of liberal violence towards conservatives continues unabated, and there is a wealth of videos online to prove it. However, if a conservative channel is growing in popularity through the reporting of these facts, such videos are quickly removed. The irony is that liberals should be correcting their own behaviour, instead of censoring people who expose such deplorable actions.

Of course, this guideline is not only about turning people away from the truth, but to condition the mind of the public. It is because of Youtube's overzealous policy of censoring violence and the truth, which has turned a whole generation into snowflakes who lurk in safe spaces. These quisling puppets can no longer tolerate what they consider as distressing images. Whether it be of video game footage where a male character hits a woman, a liberal is naturally triggered. Take for example Youtuber 'Shirrako', whom uploaded a couple of videos of his character punching a feminist NPC (non playable character) in game. While the content is certainly trivial and immature, the liberal community pounced on the opportunity to shut down the gamer's channel who had amassed over 500k followers. Within days, other liberal gamers were celebrating the censorship, much the same way as the Hitler youth celebrated their Fuhrer's decision to put Jews in the camps. And this was just over a video game. This goes to show how the weaponisation of gender politics and the #metoo movement has spread throughout every facet of our lives, that even the innocent video game is not safe. But this was all by design to create red lines to control society. If the youth actually used their brains once in a while, they would realise that they were being manipulated for a diabolical agenda.

IMPERSONATION

Identity theft is no joke, but neither is Youtube's unjustified termination of accounts which celebrate conservatives through 'mirroring'. How the guideline now works is quite simple. If a conservative has been suspended from the platform, then no other user can re-upload the former Youtuber's content through a fan-based channel. This would be considered as identity impersonation. Once again, Google has you cornered. Once you're excommunicated from the online community, no-one will ever hear from you again. Communist Russia and China were and are notorious for this behaviour. Today, this is just another red line emulated by Silicon Valley which all must be careful of. Finally, the guideline is somewhat broad as it also applies to political critics who might impersonate a politician through comic relief. This also is not tolerated, as the act somewhat falls between bullying and impersonation - a double whammy.

THREATS AND CHILD SAFETY

We have learned that Youtube certainly doesn't care if pedophiles run rampant on their platform, while earning money from the ad revenue system. Yet, as masters of the universe, the tech elites believe that threats and child endangerment should be defined as exposure to 'hateful' content, ie. conservatives who obstinately refuse to comply with liberal doctrine. For example, it was perfectly acceptable for liberals to upload the video of deranged actor Peter Fonda calling for migrants to rape Baron Trump. But if a conservative reported this disgusting act, their channel would be demonetized or terminated. Again, the 'bullying' guideline also overlaps this rule, as Fonda would be deemed to be a victim of online harassment.

'Child safety' is an umbrella term and can be applied to channels which advocate the second amendment and Christian homeschooling. It could also be construed as in breach if said child is educated with the real truth about political scams such as evolution, climate change, transgenderism and other liberal beliefs or dogmas. To deny a child the 'privilege', or liberal virtue of learning about how to change their sex or circumambulating around the Ka'aba, is now a child safety issue. Make no mistake, the more we resist, the more they will ramp up the authoritarianism. They will come for your children, mark my words.

NUDITY OR SEXUAL CONTENT

This guideline has nothing to do with protecting children from harmful imagery such as pornography or sexually explicit content. The definition has evolved into something more sinister. Today, conservative channels which demonstrate what a real man and woman should look like, are now in breach of this guideline. Content which overly supports heterosexual relationships or imagery over homosexual, are also in the firing line. After all, we're living in a 'diverse' world now, where both sexual orientations ostensibly must be represented equally. Of course, we all know that the latter has the power to destroy conservative opinion.

With this guideline, it's not uncommon for entire channels to be removed for promoting normality in sexual relationships, and preserving natural beauty, Youtube can, and will flagrantly exercise this guideline as a weapon to censor conservatives. Moreover, the term 'man' and 'woman' might also be considered a violation of the guidelines, due to gender non-binary politics. In truth, the liberal elite detest referential and unbiased content, and will resort to the 'sexual content' guideline to punish those who speak the truth. By keeping a nation in the dark, and ever feeding on propaganda, allows the overlords to create a malleable flock of useless idiots. And without comparable imagery to support an alternative thesis, explains why people today are becoming more uglier. To show an image of an attractive slim woman is now considered as 'fat-shaming', which breaches the 'sexual content', and 'bullying' guideline. Thus it's perfectly acceptable for a scantily-clad, shaved-head, morbidly obese woman to dominate a magazine cover, while covered in grotesque tattoos. Hooray for feminism! For liberals, this is virtuous. But from considering the aforementioned information, this madness was all by design to stop humans from reproducing.

On the subject of cultural sterilization, the political nerve centre today is steeped in the transgender movement which was designed to confuse our youth. For with confusion comes control. If Youtube truly wanted to stop lewd content, they would have already banned half of the music industry's videos, such as hip hop, Katie Perry, Nicki Minaj, Madonna and especially imagery of Miley Cyrus' worn out rent-a-vagina. But they haven't, because these videos invariably feature lesbian imagery and transexual themes. These corporate whores were manufactured to serve a purpose to confuse, and sexualise children, to keep the Silicon Valley culture entrenched in pedophilia, and to rob the innocence from our kids.

The actual purpose of these guidelines were to create a failsafe to stop conservatives discussing the truth about gender politics and the popularised self-genital-mutilation scam; and I'm not talking about Islamic FGM. What we are seeing today is mass hedonism and sexual depravity which is celebrated as cultural enrichment or enlightenment. Hundreds of years ago, we had the renaissance. But today, liberals truly believe they are forging "peoplekind's" destiny the same way as Leonardo Davinci did. Oh, how delusional the fools are. I weep for the future.

HARMFUL OR DANGEROUS CONTENT

While many will say that this guideline was cooked up by some overly-neurotic liberal snowflake, the real truth behind this is more subversive. Indeed, the term 'harmful and dangerous' was a title I considered for this book, but Youtube's definition was created to serve as an umbrella term to control the masses.

What the heck does harmful mean anyway these days, considering how much accepted garbage is on the internet? Hot chilli is certainly harmful if you eat too much, as are the risks in getting a tattoo. But I suppose it's not dangerous to tell a child it's perfectly safe to have a hack doctor mess with their genitals to be culturally accepted. Nonetheless this kind of content not only exists on Youtube, it's received the liberal seal of approval. Thus it's certainly evident that the guideline was solely created to get society fearing conservative ideals and beliefs, causing liberals to curl up in the foetal position.

Whether it's a hunting channel demonstrating how to skin a dead catfish, to hunt for elk, or a patriot's channel showing you how to clean your rifle, these traditions are now against the communist party policy, i.e liberals. In truth, Silicon Valley doesn't want men to be men. They want genderless, malleable puppets, with no patriarchal leaning, spouse, or balls; and certainly without any opinion. A perfect stooge. Of course, you can imagine what really is considered the most harmful and dangerous content online. It's the truth.

TONE OF VOICE

Yes, you read this correctly - your tone of voice is now a threat to the delicate ears of Silicon Valley. Draconian rules such as these are invariably created whenever the ruling elite cannot answer basic questions, or have no argument. It is also a countermeasure against dissent, and used as a subtle form of passive indoctrination through basic dog psychology. The more people curb their 'tone' lest they offend or lose their social credit, the more they become unaware of their growing compliance.

While it's undoubtable that the ghouls in the high tower will include this ridiculous guideline in their already bloated list, it inevitably will become grafted together with either the 'bullying' or 'harmful and dangerous content' as a temporary stop-gap. In regards to Youtube, I do have it on good authority from an inside source that Youtube is already devising an umbrella guideline to apply this in a broad spectrum throughout the network. While my source wishes to remain anonymous, I can tell you that the company is ramping up with its online control, and tightening its grip on the community, specifically through this guideline.

And while it may sound ridiculous to censor someone's tone of voice, sadly this is the reality of the internet today. This rule is the last piece of the liberal puzzle, which will guarantee worldwide compliance, lest people lose their online accounts, banking access, and coming social credit. Those who will literally raise their voice in frustration and protest will be deemed as 'hateful' people, whom private banking companies can purge from their services. Evidently, it's a passive aggressive form of bullying to force people to display a servile manner to the fascists in Silicone Valley. While many will doubt the applicability of this new rule, we can only refer to the leaked memo 'The Good Censor' which explicitly states that this is to become state policy. Within years, we will begin to hear the once redundant yet cringeworthy chants of dictatorial regimes…

"Papers please, line up here for social credit, and don't forget to smile."

COPYRIGHT

The copyright takedown initiative is one loophole that has been exploited, which has left us open to being attacked by many malicious entities. While the system was designed to allow copyright holders the right to takedown their intellectual property if it is improperly published, it also allows fake accounts to pose as the original holder. This is a major loophole, as only three strikes after bogus complaints can suspend a channel. In reality, any malicious troll could inflict havoc on a Youtuber through deception. All it takes is for a user to fill out three online forms, lie profusely by stating that the material is under copyright, refer the footage to some obscure DVD listed on Amazon, and presto! If successful, your channel and account is suspended. This is how low Muslims and liberals were stooping to, in an attempt to shut my channel down.

I recall our first bogus copyright claim, which was filed by some mouth-breather who posed as the infamous Wafa Sultan. You might remember her as the feisty Syrian lady who tore shreds off the Islamic establishment on live TV; which is precisely the clip we uploaded. She was also the author of 'A God Who Hates'. The claim we received indeed placed a strike on our channel, and opened our eyes to the vulnerabilities that Youtuber's face. Thus we were forced to track down the original copyright owner. The video actually belonged to the esteemed Daniel Pipes, who is the president of the Middle East Forum, and publisher of its Middle East Quarterly journal. An exceptionally brilliant man, who I might add was fabulously supportive that he actually engaged a lawyer on our behalf to take on the online troll. After all, copyright claims are no joke, and once signed, they become a legal document. Pipes didn't have to really get involved with this incident, but he showed integrity and support which I have seen missing in most so-called opponents of Islam. For that, I thank you Mr Pipes, and wish you luck in the future.

While we supplied documentation to prove that Daniel Pipes owned the copyright, Youtube ignored it for weeks, in hopes that another copyright or community strike would be added. It was clear that the ghouls were trying everything they could to derail the channel which was gaining views in the tens of millions. I wouldn't be surprised if the fake copyright claim was filed by some outsourced Youtube staff living in India. After all, the majority of Youtube's communities department are based in that region, predominantly in Muslim areas.

Nonetheless, there is one defence a channel can exercise in the case of a genuine copyright claim, which is fair use. And to indemnify themselves, Youtube itself has also acknowledged its legal responsibility to facilitate counter claims under the fair use copyright. But again, their rulings are based on the whims of corrupt content managers and staff which are uneducated in the law. A clear example of this is when we received a copyright takedown notice for a video which featured a brief clip from so-called Dr. Ravi Zacharias from RZIM (RZ International Ministries). The footage was widely uploaded on other channels for years, so we believed RZIM had no problems with it. Likewise, the short sample we edited into our montage, which was only a couple of minutes, was pertinent to the topic at hand, and was well within the boundaries of fair use. As fair use states, the content must not be overly indulgent, and to be short and concise to make the documentarian's point. We satisfied these prerequisites, yet our fight was an exercise in futility. Youtube ultimately sided with him. Here's what happened.

At first, we believed that since the video was legally acceptable, the takedown must have been another bogus claim due to the former fiasco. Thus we were forced to thoroughly check the authenticity by contacting RZIM and its content manager. We checked their online staff listing, and were directed to the appropriate person, yet who knew nothing of the claim. However, he did inform us that he was no longer with RZIM, but assured us that it was probably some mistake. We then contacted RZIM again, notifying that a possible bogus claim may have been made. This time they were exceptionally rude and dismissive. A fine example of a Christian organization, I suppose. After leaving our details and the case issue with them, we were left in limbo. Nonetheless, we filed an appeal with Youtube and waited. Soon after, we were contacted back by RZIM with a perfunctory response, and this is what they had to say:

"Yes, we did file the copyright infringement request with YouTube. YouTube found it was in violation and took the video down."

What really disappointed us was that RZIM didn't even have the guts to take full responsibility. Instead, they had to blame it on 'Youtube', despite them filing the claim. If not, they would have simply said that they, as RZIM, believed it was in violation, which provoked them to apply. Nonetheless, we contacted them again in hopes that they may remove the copyright. After all, it would be the Christian thing to do, right?

"Hello RZIM,
We never monetized the video, and I believe that the video was used under fair use, but nonetheless we respect your decision to remove it. However, we sadly have received a copyright strike and are wondering if you could retract the claim. We have no desire to reupload the video, and will keep it removed. Receiving strikes jeopardizes our channel, which has been around for almost 2 years, and we would be very grateful if you could retract the strike. I'm sure you understand it would be the Christian thing to do.

I'm not sure if you're aware, but the exact video is uploaded on many other channels, of which have not been taken down by your company. This is the reason why we uploaded the video in the first place, as we assumed your company did not mind sharing your videos on social media. Again, the following videos have already been uploaded for many years, some going as far back as 2013. We're wondering why you specifically chose our channel?"

We never received a reply. The hypocrisy is that the exact same video exists online today on many other channels, and they still haven't been taken down. It's undoubtable that we were singled out by this alleged Christian organisation because the globalist stooge as Zacharias is, didn't like the tone of my channel, or the fact that I had published a book criticising Muhammad. After all, it's no secret now that Zacharias is cozying up with the Muslim community, all the while Islamic countries are cutting Christians' heads off. But this is to be expected from an institution like so many others, which have sold their souls to the devil for thirty pieces of silver. Certainly, for a man to monetise God's word, it's no stretch for him to allegedly fake his credentials. In 2017, Christianity Today reported accusations that Zacharias had exaggerated his credentials, as there is allegedly no evidence of the man teaching at Oxford and Cambridge, or ever receiving a doctorate.

Of course, the stench of hypocrisy continues to follow this man around. In 2018, he was allegedly involved in a sexting scandal with Canadian ministry supporter, Lori Anne Thompson. I could go into this in depth, but you make your mind up. It's my opinion that Zacharias is nothing more than the Deepak Chopra of the Christian world. A man who sells each sacred letter in 'God' for a nickel. In all seriousness, Zacharias may have his sins, as we all do, but I would have appreciated that the man showed a little backbone and contact us like a real man to address RZIM's hypocrisy and targeting of our company. Instead, he simply hid behind some lackey like some underhanded, soulless bureaucrat. Sadly, RZIM only proves that the church has sold out, and are drinking from a filthy cup of fornication served by ungodly people.

With friends like these, who needs enemies. Just think how many Muslims that video could have reached, and how they could have been brought to my book to learn the truth. But so-called Christians like Zacharias, who shield Muslims away from the truth, are sadly just another censorship tool used by the ruling elite, for a great ecumenical purpose. But this was Youtube's plan all along. Align with fake Christians, and encourage an environment of illegitimate copyright takedowns while ignoring fair use. Thus we can see that this loophole is now weaponised to silence those who are considered 'hateful' and 'inconvenient'. It has nothing to do with copyright. It's just a front for useful idiots like Zacharias to hide behind.

MALIGNING MY CHARACTER

In 2018, our company decided to shut down our ebook service on the website due to lack of traffic after Google's search manipulation tactics and Youtube's banning of our channel. To add insult to injury, Google would not allow visitors access to our website through their search listings, as the message would appear stating that our site was 'unsafe' and tantamount to a 'scam'.

To combat this, we deliberately changed the metadata on the domain name to say "Google is banning this site! - Type jksheindlin.com to manually enter." Within minutes, Google's search listing immediately allowed visitors to enter and never updated the new metadata to be shown. This only proved that someone behind scenes knew they had been caught manipulating the data and access.

It is obvious that Big Tech are stuck in a quandary about how to approach my online presence. I haven't crossed the 'hate speech' line, nor am I political. The last resort they have is maligning my character as a spammer and scammer. We have sought legal advice over this and our lawyers are prepared to take this further. But we shall wait patiently to see how far this progresses.

THE DEMONETISATION TACTIC

As mentioned, after opening our channel just around the time the Syrian war and migration crisis began, we gathered immense support. It was through our channel that my book was able to reach millions through manual advertising. We had no other option but to take these proactive steps in reaching out to the public via viral video, especially when every media outlet and so-called anti-Islam activist had snubbed us.

Through Youtube's then lax monetisation standards, the revenue our channel accrued was enough to keep expanding our business and reaching out to more people than before. We truly believed we were making a difference. This all came to an end when Youtube dropped the hammer when the 'Adpocalypse' fiasco occurred. This was brought about when corporations allegedly complained that their ads were being displayed on 'far right' videos. No doubt, they meant our channel, as we had roughly over 60 million views at the time. The days of earning money through Youtube advertising was now finally at an end. Like us, hundreds, if not not thousands of Youtube creators went bust through the sudden draconian censorship placed on the network. It was obvious that corporate blackmail had nothing to do with the issue. The truth was that Google's manifesto for a 'cleaner' internet through political correctness was paramount to the corporation. It was Youtube who pulled the plug on advertising, not the advertisers.

Many people believe that it was my channel which was one of the major contributors to the Youtube Adpocalypse fiasco. Even if that was true, it exposed how liberally biased corporations were. However, I do not believe it to be so. If anything, big name brands relish having their product marketed to millions of potential customers, conservative or liberal. No company would ever cut fifty percent from their customer base. That would be suicide. In truth, companies couldn't give a damn about political correctness, as cash is the bottom line. The real culprit is Google. A pernicious, self-imploding, political beast, which believes it has the moral superiority to mould the world to its standards.

Again, I still maintain that Youtube pulled the plug on frivolous monetisation of videos to clamp down on alt-right videos taking advantage of their advertising system. It is because my channel and book had reached millions world-wide, which is the sole reason for Youtube's decision to go on the offensive. In reality, it was no-one's fault of the conservative aligned, as it was destined to occur regardless, due to the liberal's growing position on intolerance towards academic diversity. What is even more telling, is that our channel must have made Google literally hundreds and millions of dollars in revenue, yet the company would rather destroy us, than mutually prosper. It only proves that Google is no longer interested in profit, but political indoctrination.

GUILTY BY ASSOCIATION

Not long after our channel faced the axe, it was apparent that the ghouls in the high tower were still adamant about wiping any trace of my work from their system. From what I've been told through numerous emails of disgruntled Youtube users, the corporation has actively removed any channel from promoting my book. This was not isolated to the US and EU regions, but as far as Russia. One channel named 'Sexy book club' had a Youtube channel which was banned for publicly reading my book during a video. From what I've been told, they had a substantial amount of subscribers.

The same applies to Facebook where users have been shut down for simply reposting one of my book advertisements. Because the material does not conflict with the company's community standards, the content is simply deemed as 'spam and misleading'. This only proves that the big four have conspired in a coup to malign and erase my presence. But again, this liberal tactic is part and parcel of the Marxist hive-mind. Much like the former KGB era, where dissidents are tracked, hunted and shut down, it's happening again today. Not even the president is safe, as they've targeted Trump for three years with the Russian witch-hunt. What is evident is that they'll continue to keep this up until all dissidents are stopped.

CLOSING THE DOORS ON FREEDOM

After all the strikes, the appeals, the online fight to stay public, we still managed to beat the system - for a while. But it wasn't enough for the men in the high tower to see us bullied incessantly. They weren't going to give up without breaking their own rules - we had to be silenced permanently.

Oddly enough, while the noose was firmly placed around our channel's neck, it was still gaining around 1.5 million views a month, plus a steady subscriber following of around 1500 people also a month. This must have infuriated the ghouls to no end. Despite them moving the goalpost further away, we still persevered. No matter what they threw at us, nothing could stick. When people become desperate, they resort to desperate measures and most often ignore the standards they set forth.

In 2018, after two successful years of reaching out to millions of people, Youtube pulled the plug. After throwing community strikes and demonetization our way, they turned to the only thing they could use to get rid of us - the lie. Ultimately, Youtube conjured up fictitious charges based on biased speculation without any evidence. In a move of sheer vindictiveness, and after 71 million visitors, NBT Zone and its entire contents were removed for allegedly violating 'spam and misleading content'. No strikes were given. Just years of work flushed down the toilet to please the liberal elites. Despite a complete lack of evidence, it didn't matter. They hold the keys to the internet, so who would dare challenge them?

I believe their defence will rely on the bogus testimonies of disgruntled Muslims who have for the last few years screamed that my book is 'all lies', despite never having read it. But this is just the cover story. The truth lies in politics, population control and money. Islam is the linchpin in national security for all western countries. Ever since the mass introduction of the cult, it has allowed governments to spend billions in defence and counterterrorism contracts. Undoubtedly, my book has been a fly in the ointment for the elites, who wish to exploit ignorant Muslims for their own gain. If Muslims suddenly woke up to the fact their prophet was a liar and a fraud, Islam would cease to exist. This is very problematic for our disgusting civilisation who exploits wicked doctrines for financial and political gain. Undoubtedly, the real problem had nothing to do with the ostensible conservative leanings of my book, but the content's message which was spreading. My book proved to be particularly hard to censor due to the fact that the material is heavily referenced using only Islamic texts. This does not fall under 'hate speech', but academia. The catch is that if they shut down the book because it was "hateful", then they indirectly would infer that Islam was a hateful ideology. This is the conundrum when someone tries to conceal truth, and advocate the lie.

In hindsight, I believe that my banning might not have actually been a group effort, and probably was due to some disgruntled Muslim who predictably couldn't control himself, thus hitting the red button. Again, this is typical of allowing irrational, brainwashed Muslims with short tempers, to do their bidding. With one click of a mouse button, they had effectively ruined my career. This is the world we now live in. Where our employment is overruled by a select few elite, who are slowly drinking themselves to death on the poison of cultural Marxism.

BARNES AND NOBLE CENSORS MY REVIEWERS

Undoubtedly contributing to the 'spam and misleading' echo of lies circulating Silicon Valley, Barnes and Noble were allegedly caught in the act of censorship and deleting reviews. This was widely publicised on the independent news source, and now defunct 'The Muslim Issue'. B&N were discovered to have actively deleted favourable reviews praising my work.

From what I read, the original reviewer was elated in discovering through my book that Islam and psychopathy were directly linked. According to the article, the reviewer just said the truth in that Islam was the creation of a mentally-ill person. B&N objected to the content, as the review allegedly fell outside their 'community guidelines'. Thus, they removed it without any notice. However at the same, B&N allowed an identifiable firebrand Muslim's review which denigrated the book while leaving fallacious information about the contents. The Muslim reviewer also went on to vent his poison about non-Muslims, his advocation for Islam, then slandered me personally.

After being exposed, some of the original reviews were reinstated, but we are still unsure of how far this has gone, or the damage done. Interestingly, if you were to search for this article, it appears to have been deleted, along with the owner's website. Trace elements of the website's articles can be found on Reddit and Twitter, but alas all content has been removed. We suspect that this was due to the hosting company Wordpress taking a firm stance on anti-Islam content, which is ironic as the company is staunchly in your face with their LBGT values. And we all know how Muslims feel about homosexuals.

Review manipulation is actually nothing new. Most book retailers have been caught in this deceptive practice, and I have the screenshots to prove it. On average, we estimate roughly that for every three positive reviews, they delete one. This is obviously done to deter customers and to deceive the public into believing that my book sales have not been entirely successful as I claim. But, like I said, I have the screenshots and data to prove otherwise.

My advice to my readers is to check your reviews to see if they're still online. Chances are a good majority have been removed.

DISQUS CENSORS ME

For the layman, Disqus is an online comment platform which is integrated into a wealth of online news websites. Just another outfit straight from the communist nerve centre called Silicon Valley. Its crime is also curating the truth, and removing people's comments on a whim. Just visit my website and see for yourself the greatest hits which Disqus has removed. Moreover, the company allegedly also admits it spies on users. This is why I've coined the new name 'Disqusting'.

Disqus is one of the many social media companies that somehow hides behind the technicality that they're not actually a part of the big four. But in a sense, they are. They're fully integrated into many Google listed websites, and are utilized by Facebook, Twitter and others. The company cannot deny its intimate involvement with Big Tech, as its platform allows users to sign in with third-party accounts from Facebook and Google. It just shows they all share an incestuous relationship, and avoid blatant antitrust by delegating niche markets among themselves, but indeed they do conspire and act together as one whole unit. In reality, like the big four, Disqus is just another outfit working at the behest of the cultural elite. It's clearly just another tag and bag operation.

By artificially guiding the public conversation, Disqus is no different than the rest. It is an unforgivable act to turn the volume down on some people, while allowing others to speak. There is certainly a special place in hell for the arrogant who believe they have the moral superiority to silence people. The danger involved in manipulating the conversation, is that history has proven those who advocate one-sided debate and political bias, will usher in the construction of ghettos, gulags, concentration camps, and the start of a holocaust. Hitler was no stranger to guiding the national conversation, and he did so with ease as he had the majority control. Today, it's clear that Disqus is moulding the world's conversation. By removing certain people from a group, you'd be surprised how quickly the narrative can change for the worse, and how lines can be drawn to persecute those without a voice.

I wouldn't be surprised in a few years if conservatives will be made to display identifiable tags on their accounts, just like how the Jews were made to wear the star of David on their arms. Perhaps it will be applied in reverse. For all to live in the 'new world', we must be forced to wear a mark to be even allowed to speak. Of course, I'm referring to the biblical 'mark of the beast', which looks inevitable with the current political climate of Big Tech silencing people.

Like the big four, Disqus has also taken the fascist proactive stance to usher in Marxism by banning many platforms such Alex Jones' Infowars. Jones warned of what we are experiencing, by coining the term 'Chi-coms' while referring to the Chinese influenced monolith tech companies of today, of which is certainly occurring. Interestingly, the following referenced excerpt from Disqus' Wikipedia page gives an insight into how Big Tech works.

> "Disqus does moderate communities which use its service, by **treating some comments as spam, when clearly they are not**, in other words, **it censors political comment**, possibly by key word detection, leading to controversial moderation in some communities."

I rest my case.

THE CANADIAN FEDERATION OF LIBRARY ASSOCIATIONS CENSORS ME

In a shocking move towards state censorship, Canada has advocated the complete ban of my book from their bookshelves. In 2016, the Canadian Federation of Library Associations tabled the motion to pull my book from all libraries throughout the nation. The document which was circulated in the government was called "Inappropriate for Any Age – Ban It Forever!" Apparently, the brief refers to my book as illicit, contraband, and has grouped it together with other soon to be censored books. Ladies and gentlemen, this is nothing short of the state book-burning we witnessed under Nazi Germany's tyrannical rule.

What is even more baffling, is that the CFLA never bothered to actually read the contents of my book which does not present a case for offensiveness. More to the point, even if it did, no state organisation has the right to withhold literature from anyone. The irony is that you can readily purchase Hitler's 'Mein Kampf' on Amazon and have it shipped to or printed locally in Canada, but somehow my book is more dangerous than the mind of an anti-semitic madman who murdered six million Jews. Taking this into consideration, I don't think it's unfeasible that Canada will soon have its first annual book-burning event to purge political liabilities. The Nazis started with censorship, and we all know how that turned out - 60 million people dead by 1945.

Of course, this is not surprising considering that the current Prime Minister of Canada, Justin Trudeau, is wholly aligned and controlled by a heavy Muslim constituency and parliament. Most of his chief advisors are Muslims, where they saw the introduction of the broadsword 'hate speech' bill which prevents people such as myself and patriots the right to speak up against the cult. Naturally, this bill wasn't introduced to protect all faiths, but predominantly Islam. On a more positive note, it seems that Trudeau's popularity has plummeted after his heavy-handed approach towards conservative dissidents and his constant mosque carpet-kissing antics. It is evident that the nepotist has indeed introduced a number of Sharia compliant laws which are beginning to cause friction in the greater community. The municipal government of Huntingdon has financed Islam by building a local mosque and Halal slaughterhouse with state money, and gave a one-year property tax break to attract more Muslim residents. Likewise, the municipal government of Edmonton also has ruled that men cannot swim at the public school during certain hours of the week, to be in compliance with Sharia law while Muslim women swim. Welcome to Canada.

"We need to make sure that we are working with communities, like the Muslim community, for example, to demonstrate that Islam is not incompatible with free and open western societies."
- Justin Trudeau, Canadian Prime Minister, CBC on January 31, 2016

Islam is not incompatible with free and open western societies, Justin? Then why is my book being banned from all libraries throughout your country? As far as I know, Islam is the only religion in the world that pressures governments through intimidation to use censorship to cover up the nasty truth about their cult. But alas, this is the state of Canada today.

As far as I know, my book is the first anti-Islam publication in Canadian history to be attacked and placed under a permanent ban, by the CFLA. I'm honoured and disgusted at the same time! Again, there is a special place in hell for Trudeau to burn.

MY FIGHT WITH DISTRIBUTION COMPANIES

While being ruthlessly persecuted by Big Tech from all sides, I was also subject to harassment and probing through my book distributors. Due to the controversial nature of my book, I have never given any private information to my publisher or any distribution company. This was an agreement that was set in stone from the first day I published. As far as they cared, as long as the book sold, they were happy. That all changed when by book became a bestseller, and was obviously ruffling some feathers within the liberal inner circles and Islamic community.

Within weeks, my distributors pushed for me to disclose my personal address and contact details. This was highly unorthodox and unethical considering the contract we agreed to. Even worse, they threatened that if I didn't comply, the company would lock my publisher and myself out of the account system until I could 'prove' who I was. After pursuing through their terms and conditions, there was nothing that could permit them taking such draconian steps. Our contention is that the tech elites had pushed their inner circle to phish for information, and eventually flush me out. It didn't work.

Legally speaking, they didn't realise that I was using an overseas proxy to handle my affairs and act as representative. Not surprisingly, one of our major distributor's European headquarters are based in south England, near London. That whole area has become a hotbed of radical Islam and no-go zones that the government and crooked media turns a blind eye to. I wouldn't be surprised if half of their staff are employed by Muslims, considering that it is now frowned upon by companies to hire 'white British' nationals.

This incident woke us up to the fact that the west is no longer a free civilization, but now a Marxist playground for thuggish technocrats who exploit Muslims to act as their personal henchmen.

THE WAR ON FREEDOM

With Big Tech reaping your data, and the World Wide Web being setup to track digital fingerprints, it is inevitable that actual crime or *perceived* crimes are envisioned to become impossible to commit. For the former, this is a good thing. But for the latter, it's entirely disturbing. As history dictates, since the killing of JFK, there has been palpable distrust in our governments. Moreover when only 45 days after 9/11, the Patriot Act was introduced which gives authorities the power to remove citizens at will, all on trumped up charges and vague suspicion. While the elites have argued that the act was created to catch terrorists, in reality, it turns regular citizens into suspects. 9/11 was the peak era when Big Tech had reached critical mass. By then, CIA and NSA had funded untold numbers of private groups. Only four years before the worst terrorist attack in history, Google was just a nascent company relying solely on government grants. And this is where history takes a dark turn. Many people believe that it was 9/11 which inevitably changed the world. But in my humble opinion, the event only played a part in the catalyst which would bring about world control. The real milestone for modern human slavery was the invention of accelerated machine learning, and Google's advanced search and track algorithms. The rest, as they say, is history.

For over twenty years, we saw a culmination of the worst kinds of atrocities lead by Muslim radicals. But in truth, these were nothing but coordinated attacks by a deep state, all used to usher in a globalist agenda. Ask yourself, if Big Tech has the intel on every citizen on this planet, and the intelligence community still manages to let slip a few terrorist attacks a year, why do you think this happens? The end goal is to usher in more global security, more cameras, more government grants for cyber security, data trawling and social engineering. In academia, we call this Hegelian Dialectics, or cause and effect. For example, the government secretly introduces a calcium counter-agent into the water supply, causing our teeth to become brittle. Consequently, the natural reaction is for the authorities to advocate fluoride intake in school lunches, causing sterilization. Islam is the counter-agent, government overreach is the fluoride.

This has been happening for years, and when you start to study world politics and the dirty games they play, you become tuned to the disgusting globalist psyche. The more you begin to realize, the more you communicate your suspicions. This alone also triggers the Hegelian Dialectic effect, which provokes liberals to introduce the term 'hate speech'. This is the war we are facing today. It's no longer bullets and shrapnel, but purely psychological tactics. And with their agenda becoming even more conspicuous day by day, we're still losing the battle through global censorship. Political correctness has become fully weaponized, and is no longer employed solely to make everyone feel accepted. It allows Big Tech in collaboration with the intelligence community, to clamp down on dissidents and political liabilities, i.e conservatives, Christians and libertarians.

While spying on private citizens has proven to be exceptionally lucrative for Alphabet Inc. the beast has taken on a more menacing form. Today, Google's services are slowly enveloping our life, from planning, shopping, banking, dating, thinking, and more. If you can think it, Google will give you the answer, thus controlling your mind. However, all of these system protocols are based on political thought, not popularity. In other words, the system has been rigged to create a Marxist utopia to control your life, down to the last insignificant detail, much like the former days of the soviet union. And this is how the enemy wins the war, by manipulating the populous.

We can already see the preliminary signs of Google's Marxist corporate control and its influence on users. The entire tech ecosystem is ostensibly calibrating itself around your lifestyle, but in fact is wholly moulding your thought patterns through a number of psychological tactics. Mobility, sociality, politics, recreation, education, cultural osmosis and linguistics are all being subtly altered to remove you from your former self. You might not realise it, but over time, your entire life might be affected to the point where you don't even know who you are anymore.

For example, Google might at some point calculate your ride to work based on the most 'safest' route, to avoid lower socio-economic areas which reflect on liberal government negligence. The system might also organise your friends based on liberals trends and political beliefs, shunning those who have been deemed as liabilities over 'hate speech'. Through this, the online social ecosystem might indeed recommend desirable social groups based on Google's reasoning, which of course, would mean no conservatives. Likewise, to complete Big Tech's social engineering program, your account might be recommended with a number of prospective partners and spouses who are desirable to the liberal echo chamber, and based on your current social credit ranking. If that's not scary enough, I would envision that the Google ecosystem would also encourage you to listen to anti-American, liberal musicians which are slowly brainwashing you through Marxist rhetoric. They would also discourage you from watching certain alternative movies through manipulated fake reviews, and fabricated lies. Finally, your linguistics are already coming under attack through Big Tech's aggressive grammar and spell-check feature.

It's helpful to be corrected, but when the system starts pedantically changing your grammar to suit the liberal narrative, it's worrying.

In short, linguistics are heavily tied to psychology. There has been much study into the effects that language plays on our minds. For example, the "Sapir-Whorf hypothesis," is a well-founded theory which states that language isn't just a way to communicate, but it also influences or even determines those thoughts. And moreover, the evolution of a language is moulded by the culture and environment its speakers live in, which would mean a cyclical effect. I believe that Big Tech is employing these tactics to mess with the populous' minds, for their benefit. The changes might be incremental now, but after careful curation, and subtle manipulation, the system will mould you to be more compliant.

Hitler and Stalin were masters of controlling the masses through subtle measures as the aforementioned. In the west, we've been lucky to be divorced from such tyrannical, underhanded standards. But in the last ten years, we've seen a surge in advocation of such principles. Like Hitler's Gestapo, and Stalin's Stasi, your entire life and its secrets, are all kept on record for the ruling elite to peruse through without your consent. And there is no way to find exactly how far they've burrowed in, or if there's anyway to permanently delete your sensitive data. Insider sources to Google and the big four have already stated that even though you might think you are deleting your account, your data is never actually erased, but deeply archived for future leverage.

Think about it, all your past and current bank details, relationships, social affiliations, permanent records, sexual habits, your ex-wife's underwear size, personal vices, taxes, hidden bank accounts, your children's private data, all sitting somewhere in a Big Tech server with an NSA backdoor, just waiting to be exploited once the globalists seize power to purge dissidents from existence. This is Orwellian citizen monitoring at critical mass. And with Google's current trend of seek and destroy towards conservatives, and other political enemies, it's only going to get worse.

THE DIABOLICAL SYSTEM OF CONTROL

The plan is so sinister, it's ingenious. Google and the Big Tech four have setup a system where people willingly give up their data, by feeding on the growing trend of narcissism. And this is why Hollywood seduced people for over forty years - to make them believe the lie that someday, they'll be famous. The more people become lovers of themselves, the more they share and the more Google profits. Ultimately, the more the deep state government knows about you. It's a sociological fact that people are feeling more disconnected, more depressed if they don't have at least one million subscribers, followers, or friends. It is people's inherent pride which has locked them in a digital prison planet, and in a sense, subscriptions, followers, friend counts, are the official social credit score. In this sick tech culture, the mentality dictates that if you have no followers, you're not trustworthy. This cultural paradigm shift could indeed have a long lasting impact on banking, loans, and purchasing of food. Private industries are already shunning conservatives and anyone they deem undesirable, i.e those with no social credit, or blacklisted digital social history. They used to call it 'street cred', but today it's taken a turn into a dark alley.

The culprits in Silicon Valley are far and wide. Apple itself has fostered an elitist culture based on its ecosystem, where customers line up for days to get the latest phone, which is virtually identical to the last model. Those who are not up with the latest, feel somehow disconnected and found wanting. In a desperate act of reaching for relevancy, we have youth literally camping outside at the Apple store for the latest craze. This hysteria then sees more gullible fools obsess and join the fickle cause. It's like slaves lining up to enter the death camp. The tragedy is that whatever major additions are added, like facial recognition scanning, ID fingerprinting, financial consolidation through Apple Pay, have all been introduced to control your life and spy on you. In fact, only recently, Apple introduced the 'trust score' system in their ecosystem to weed out those who are unfit to communicate and share their ideas. Of course, the monolith downplays this feature as merely an 'improvement', like biometrics, to help trustworthy people connect, i.e liberals.

The reality is that these 'improvements' are just another way to shackle you to the plantation. Not surprisingly, this tech trend of subservience is not reserved only for Apple. Google is also guilty with its Android phone system. However, Google is by far the most diabolical of the bunch, as it encourages all other mobile phone manufacturers to use Android alone. Nonetheless, they all work together to reap your data, personal measurements, facial characteristics and voice - all to use against you in the near future.

When Gmail was first released, its primary pitch was that you'd never have to delete your emails ever again to save space. It was and always has been unlimited in data storage. The 'unlimited' keyword was the bait that the masses took, where all signed up and willingly gave their life to the NSA; again all for the sake of convenience. It's staggering to think that if we were to calculate just how much personal data and correspondence has been sent through Gmail since its creation, we would be theoretically stacking office paper sheets to the moon and back again, five times over. This is how much information the government has on us. And they never lifted a finger to pry into your life. You just served it up on a plate. In reality, Big Tech masquerades as hubs of innovation but the truth is that they're just pernicious spy agencies. And with our entire lives being recorded by the minute, it's all going to come down to whether you are a dissident, or an asset for the system.

If anyone is to doubt the government's involvement in the great tech agenda, I encourage all to do a simple search on the internet to see Obama's meeting in the White House with Big Tech leaders. Virtually every single CEO was representing each company over a champagne dinner. What they actually discussed is unknown. But what is obvious, is that after that meeting, Obama took measures to relinquish regulation of ICANN - Internet Corporation for Assigned Names and Numbers. Basically, the company which runs domain names and their data. Traditionally, the US government is to oversee this department, lest it be infiltrated for nefarious deeds. Naturally, to complete the new world agenda, Obama gave up that duty, and let the agency run autonomously. ICANN now operates above any international law, and is accountable only to itself. All thanks to Obama. Thus we have seen people's domains come under attack for free speech. The agency now has the power without US regulation or public oversight, to rule the internet. It can turn off anyone's domain who are deemed liabilities, and most importantly, they can expose private data under the Patriot Act. This is beyond Orwellian, and is a travesty in a western country. It is obvious that this was highly coordinated, as we now know that Obama was already spying on Trump before he ran for office. He knew that if Trump ever rose to power, they would need a plan to censor conservatives without US regulation and oversight. ICANN's sudden departure from US regulation proves that it was a preemptive move to corner the political arena. Of course, this was necessary for a man who desired to cover up his controversial secret homosexual life. For a man who boasted that his administration never had any scandals, the truth is quite the contrary.

While the press has desperately covered up Obama's past, latent and leaked sources still in the deep recesses of the internet have proven that Obama was indeed a protege of Satanist and Marxist, Saul Alinksky. Alinsky, the author of 'Rules for radicals' dedicated his book to Lucifer in the first few pages. According to Alinsky biographer Sanford Horwitt, US President Barack Obama was influenced by Alinsky and followed in his footsteps as a Chicago-based community organizer. Horwitt asserted that Barack Obama's 2008 presidential campaign was heavily influenced by Alinsky's teachings. For three years in the mid 80s, Obama worked for the Developing Communities Project, which was influenced by Alinsky's work, where he wrote an essay that was collected in a book memorializing Alinsky.

This is why the internet has turned into a constrictive landscape, where free speech is quickly diminishing. Obama's legacy has been influenced by the prince of this world, Satan.

THE CREATION OF A POLICE STATE

On December 31, 2011, Obama signed the **National Defense Authorization Act** (**NDAA**) into law (now named the John McCain NDAA) which in addition to allocating $662 billion to the Pentagon, also contained a measure which **allows US citizens to be taken**

into custody and held indefinitely without ever being charged with a crime. Not only can any citizen deemed a threat to "national security interests of the United States" be held forever without receiving a trial, the military itself will retain the power to arrest citizens. While many will doubt the extent of this law's power, we must remember that since 9/11, the US has indefinitely remained in a state of war, which grants the government licence to detain individuals under court martial, if necessary.

NDAA Section 1022, subsection (c) allows power of "(1) Detention under the <u>law of war</u> without trial until the <u>end of the hostilities</u> authorized by the Authorization for Use of Military Force." This information recently surfaced during the 'Clergy response team' scandal which has revealed that Christian Pastors are being groomed to brainwash congregations to give authority only to the state, and not God. This scandal illustrated how the deep state have already made plans for martial law, mass arrests under the act, and for citizens to be put in FEMA camps for processing, in the event of a 'federal emergency'. A federal emergency could actually entail a massive data breach, where libertarian hackers expose deep state corruption, or are working to establish free speech once again.

In regards to the scandal, a pastor who shall remain nameless stated that all clergy will be utilized as 'informants'. Shockingly, this alone violates the legal privilege of confidentiality between pastor and church-goer that is currently recognized by US law. What this means is that all church-goers can no longer trust the sanctity of personal confessions made to pastors, priests or rabbis. Like the internet, their conversations are to be recorded, monitored and assessed by a military presence. This kind of police state security is unprecedented, and flies in the face of what the founding fathers stood for. Nonetheless, the trend of citizen monitoring continues, as this program appears to be still active. According to sources, there are currently around 28,000 FEMA trained pastors, all who are sworn to secrecy. Disturbingly, the nameless pastor reiterated their sole mandate is to, "Calm people down and encourage their compliance within their new surroundings, and the state." Accordingly, this would mean the confiscation of arms, Bibles, and whatever means necessary to quell the masses.

THE BIGGEST CENSORSHIP SCANDAL IN HISTORY

While the reader may be shocked to hear of the USA involving itself in concentration camp style detention centres on home soil, the sad fact is that this isn't the first time Big Tech has orchestrated mass arrests and detention of private citizens. In the 1930s, IBM made the punch card system exclusively for the Nazis so that they could categorise Jews, dissidents, and libertarians; those who eventually all were gassed and incinerated. Without Big Tech, the holocaust simply would not have taken place. Mass categorisation to send citizens to labour or extermination camps is only possible through mass computing. And it was only achieved through American Big Tech's intervention. Of course, many would doubt the extent of the involvement, and pass it off as capitalistic investment. But in reality, the elites at IBM knew exactly what was happening in Germany. No country would need a mass computational system to categorise people, unless extermination was on the cards, literally. In fact, IBM CEO Thomas J. Watson met personally with Adolf Hitler in the 1930s. History proves that Watson was a high ranking freemason and was called "the world's greatest salesman", despite being complicit in the murder of millions.

While the rest of the world were unaware, except for the elites, the Nazi killing machine was desperately trying everything they could to murder as many Jews, dissidents and 'sub-humans' they could. First they started with censoring the press, then silencing the people. Then came the removal of the disabled under the Aktion T4 program, followed by the ghettos. Most Germans were unaware themselves that the government had already began a systematic process of arrest and murder by the first initial means. The Nazi's started with shooting squads by moving dissidents to the countryside, then initiated makeshift gas chambers in the back of military trucks, by poisoning citizens using carbon monoxide coming from the exhaust. When this didn't meet the daily quota, Himmler introduced the idea of using the cyanide-based pesticide 'Zyklon-B', but this time in designated death camps. Himmler actually learned about this chemical during his 'science' studies in university.

It was then that Hitler and his cronies introduced the orders for the 'final solution', where the goal was to be around 12,000 Jews exterminated a day. However, the key component that was missing for this diabolical plan of action to work, was exactly what the Americans possessed - the computer. History books show that IBM amassed incredible wealth from the Holocaust, which explains its monolithic status today. Those who could afford to purchase vast stock options in the company were undoubtedly those whose feet never touched the ground. Today, we would call them the deep state, the one percent, and the elites. Their entire family estates were built on the bones of Jews and free-thinkers. And if we witness the trend occurring today, it's clear that history is repeating.

While this may offend many veterans and patriots, it is my contention that one of the main reasons the US entered the war, was to cover up the extent of IBM's and Big Tech's involvement in murdering over six million ethnic people. While it's no secret today that an American corporate entity aided in exterminating human lives, the vast trail of evidence was ultimately destroyed to protect family legacies, the identity of those who financed Hitler's war machine, and to bury elites' secrets. If anyone is to doubt this, then one must think on how the United States entered the war, and for what reason.

If we retrospectively analyse that era, both nations were separated by an ocean, and were inconsequential to each other in world trade. History dictates that it was actually Hitler who suddenly declared war on the US, despite lack of provocation. Even today, there is still no real historical or logical reason given for Hitler's sudden decision.

Why would the dictator suddenly provoke the greatest military machine in history to enter the war? It is obvious that Hitler had inside knowledge through his network of spies, political whores, and American fifth columnists that the echelon were dead-set on covering up the vast extent of both countries crimes. This meant invasion. The American elites had to cover up what their brethren, the SS, had been carrying out, lest the USA become a world pariah for centuries. The US seized the moment to turn a bad situation into an opportunity to paint themselves as the liberators, instead of perpetrators of genocide.

Time was running out, and being the proud man Hitler was, it would be perceived to be a sign of weakness had he not declared war first. After all, he was bold enough to take on Russia in winter, which was his fatal mistake. Moreover, it is now historically obvious the man was made the sole scapegoat for the Holocaust by the American elite, and O.S.S, of which he most certainly would've predicted. Thus it was a preemptive move for Hitler to save face, as he knew the US would plan an invasion for this sole reason. It was inevitable. It is only in the last thirty years that IBM's involvement has come to the public's attention. Had the elites not seized the opportunity to cover up the extent of their crimes, I'm very sure the world would've known the truth directly after the war.

While I'm sure there are many who will rebuff this as a conspiracy theory, and you have every right to, we must remember that both the American and British establishment have a history of censoring the past for their own agendas, and for good publicity. It is only recently that information has surfaced which proves that **both the Federal Reserve and the Bank of England actually financed Nazi Germany.** This is a fact that has been publicised by the Centre for Research of Globalization. Furthermore, while this inconvenient truth backs up my contention, I must also divulge that the British establishment also covered up the fact that the abdicated King Edward VIII, had colluded with Hitler in bringing England to her knees. History now proves that the monarch indeed intended to be a puppet king for Hitler, and was enamoured with Nazism. Records state that the treacherous King had actually visited the extermination camps, with his Nazi spy mistress, Wallis Simpson. Simpson was an American who was deeply in love with the idea of a Nazi one world government. Historical records now prove that the King intended for Simpson to be co-regent under a Nazi ruled Britain. Like the rumoured to be transsexual Michelle Obama, Simpson was also certainly not a *woman* in the whole sense. This strange perversion allowed the transgender to sleep her way through the Nazi high ranks, where she funnelled information to them from Edward's pillow talk. It is also another fallacy that Edward abdicated from the throne for a 'woman'. The obvious truth is that 'the firm', the royal establishment, had discovered the monarch's intentions to collaborate with Hitler. Is it only after his forced abdication, that Hitler declared war on the UK's closest ally - America. This again would explain Hitler's desire to declare war on the US, which had become irremovably closer to the UK through the abdication.

While the war indeed ended, the truth is that Nazism did not just vanish into the history books. On the contrary. The extent of Royal and US elite ties to the Fuhrer were vast in the select blue blood circles. The American elites today are still entrenched in the same principles which Hitler advocated. This being social engineering, eugenics, censorship, big government, elitism, bureaucratic and judicial corruption, insider trading, sterilization, demonisation of the lower class, and much more. In truth, America didn't defeat the Nazis. They just moved them to the US and covered up the elites' crimes. This isn't conspiracy theory, as we already know that the American military smuggled in thousands of Nazi scientists after the war, under Operation Paperclip. It is then that we saw the rise of atomic warfare, Big Pharma, and Planned Parenthood; a genocidal institution dedicated to selective breeding.

Still, there is no surprise that the US elite engaged in genocidal activities with the Nazis. After all, the prestigious University of Yale's 'Skull and Bones' fraternity shares the exact same symbol as the SS soldiers own in Nazi Germany. They were, and are basically of the same brethren, which explains the elites' hatred for free speech and independence. In conclusion, Big Tech had certainly used Hitler like a pawn to establish their agenda, which is a unified, political Europe. The EU banking system is actually the legacy of the Nazis, as is their domestic policy. Thus we can see why Big Tech is aiding Brussels in clamping down on free speech and human rights.

Be weary of the leaders whose saccharine words might tickle your ears. They just might be of the Nazi blue blood line. Do your research.

THE BRAINWASHING MACHINE

Indeed, the key to controlling a nation is through subtle brainwashing. Hitler could not have achieved the holocaust by only categorising dissidents. He needed the ministry of propaganda to manipulate the minds of the gullible, to aid in the final solution.

"The bigger the lie, the more people will believe it."
- Adolf Hitler

It wasn't only the Nazi elites who put Jews onto the trains. The people themselves came under a spell through ear-tickling rhetoric, that they would do literally anything for the cause. Moreover, for the Jews, they too bought the lie that they would be relocated to summer camps for their safety. They should have known better.

While the dark days of Nazi Germany have gone, the remnant still remains as the elites in all western countries have learned well from their brethren, and have aligned Big media with Big Tech to dominate the political landscape. Today, we are living in an age of deceit, where truth is hounded out of town and killed in the name of liberal virtue. The legacy of Hitler's reich was passed over to the American media corp, where the CIA created the program called 'Operation Mockingbird.' The top secret operation was founded directly after the fall of Nazi Germany, and during the rise of the cold war in the 1950s. Mockingbird was, and still is, a deep state government Nazi-style umbrella contingency, initiated to control the minds of private citizens, to effectively rig elections, manipulate commerce, politics, and inevitably change American culture over the span of seventy years. Today, we are seeing the effects of the project in full scale. With the rise of biased mainstream media, and the global censorship program through Big Tech, we can understand where this is all coming from. Interestingly, news anchor Walter Cronkite, labelled the 'most trusted man in America', who was also a part of project Mockingbird, actually said that we need a world government. In an archived interview, Cronkite mocked Christians who warned about the Bible's warning of the new world order, which states it will be a Satanic invention. Quite shockingly, Cronkite then said he was proud to sit at the right hand of Satan.

Mockingbird's entire mandate is deception. For in truth, man can still reason. The term 'fake news' is the direct result of President Trump exposing the corrupt media and its virulence against the perceived maverick, and the people. But of course, the coordinated attack on Trump could not have been achieved without the help of Big Tech, just like Nazi Germany. What is axiomatically clear, is that Big Tech has become by proxy, the new media. It is *the* newspaper we turn to for news. Ask Google a question, and the sources will be bound together with liberal news to form a biased opinion. It's unnerving to think that we no longer rely on a plethora of dependable news sources like the bygone days of Edward R. Murrow in the 1940s and earlier. Instead, what we know of the world today, is reported by a collective of transient, paid-off journalists, all contributing to the Marxist echo chamber from remote locations, who feed the tech beast. And it is from this extensive bias which is seeing our freedom to choose, think and speak, slowly becoming a thing of the past. Present journalism is not about reporting the news truthfully. It's become an opportunity to spin, malign outsiders, and control the nation's thought patterns to tip the balance of power. Thus was the actual mandate of Mockingbird.

After the landslide victory of Trump in 2016, the technocrats went on the offensive. Under the guidance of Mockingbird's core principles, and loyalty to the corrupt deep state, countless articles were written to demonise middle-America as backwards and ill-educated. This itself created a vacuum for the media to work symbiotically with Google and Facebook to 're-educate' the "low informed voters", as they called us. This false rhetoric is the cover story behind why Democrats lost. Sprinkle on a bit of Russian collusion rumours, and you've got yourself a narrative to work with. In that regard, Hillary Clinton's track record of illegal pay-for-play tactics and bureaucratic criminality was thus allegedly all fake news. In the mind of a liberal, she was unfairly treated, and overdue for her natural elevation to empress. But for the rest of the country, and world, who saw her for what she truly is, they weren't buying it. With the wealth of negativity surrounding her on the internet, it's no wonder she heralded the call for censorship.

> "The internet needs an editor."
> - Hillary Clinton.

Nonetheless, billions of dollars were at stake for both the 2016 and 2020 election. Especially for Big Tech, which aggressively promoted Planned Parenthood, green energy, climate change and Hillary's promised power cabal 'selectorate', whose bitterness was evident after losing to Trump. Hillary would have promised her goons positions of enviable power, only for them to be relegated to the dark side of capitol hill and Hollywood. This in turn jumpstarted Mockingbird's protocols to ramp up the full attack on anyone who defied the liberal order. For example, the public is wholly unaware that the now defunct website 'JournoList' was created solely to coordinate attacks on Trump by networking journalists together who were funded by socialist quangos, where they were told what to write. This was nothing more than a coordinated coup through media manipulation that even Mockingbird would not dare bring itself to. But alas, this incident exemplified the pure desperation the brainwashed liberal elite harboured after losing positions of power. While JournoList has gone the way of the dodo, the legacy of media corruption lives on in the spirit of what we are experiencing today. It explains why nearly all news sources are hellbent against the President, conservatives and anyone else who goes against the grain.

The media's unhealthy infatuation and histrionics over Trump is not only because he is seemingly going against globalist policies, but for simply being independent. Trump is the line in the sand, which was drawn by the elites. It doesn't matter what he does. The mere fact that he does it, must be condemned. It sets the example for others who might be inspired to follow suit. Those who dare step forward to challenge the beast, are quickly assaulted from all sides by the media. This is now global policy. Logic would dictate that a lucrative niche market, in a saturated leftist industry, would exist in reporting alternative news, which therefore would motivate mainstream news companies to seize the opportunity. In economics, we call this hedge investing, or diversification. But this is bigger than money, this is a grab for total world power.

Under the umbrella of Mockingbird, the NGO company Media Matters for America has also worked tirelessly to censor opponents of the globalist system. In 2018, a leaked manifesto exposed the organisation for colluding with socialist and billionaire George Soros. According to The Washington Free Beacon, it obtained a "confidential" 49 page report from Media Matters for America that was presented to donors at a retreat in January 2017, just after Trump's inauguration. Inside the manifesto, the group laid out a plan to rally social media giants together, to silence conservative voices. Of course, the syllabus wasn't exactly as forthcoming as we'd expect. Hidden in pages of liberal fluff, the goals were enshrouded under typical liberal spin such as 'The top watchdog against fake news and propaganda'. Likewise, 'In a hyper fragmented media environment, the right is aggressively exploiting vulnerabilities and finding new ways to poison the information ecosystem with lies. Media Matters is there to stop them.'

One could say that the Media Matters declaration of war on conservatives is the reason why we are experiencing a full-on assault from the left in terms of censorship. The more truth we speak, the more they go on the offensive. Interestingly, the group pouts about the 'decay of journalism', when in reality, there is very little of it occurring in the left-wing media. If one was to read the manuscript, they would immediately see parallels between it and the communist manifesto. The group also implores Big Tech to ramp up the use of machine learning A.I to corner the internet, and to prevent conservatives from having a voice ever again.

But alas, even A.I's vast calculative mind wasn't enough to begin the 'clean up' of the liberal internet. It is clear that Youtube became so desperate to tie up loose ends, that they were found to be colluding with the Southern Poverty Law Centre, which was investigated and discovered to be hired as to police the internet with its 'Trusted Flaggers' force; these were employed to stamp out so-called 'hate speech' content. Sources have stated that over 30,000 people around the world, most probably from poor Islamic countries, were hired based on their ideological preferences, and to ruthlessly target conservatives. It is almost a certainty that my channel was axed because of this initiative, as we received no warning, strike or explanation. We were simply cut down in the prime of our career. The fact that Youtube had to resort to an extremist, left-wing organisation like the SPLC, was entirely confronting.

According to Youtube, the corporation continues to work with over one hundred Marxist organizations, all seeking to take down material which is abhorrent to the liberal mind. This being alternative views, and general patriotic, pro-gun and news channels. It is also evident that Facebook entered the fray with full vigour under the spell of Media Matters, as the company was discovered to have set up a 'War room', with the intention of destroying conservative presence and growth during the 2018 mid-terms. What we witnessed was a consistent purge of Christians, pro-gun and free speech activists. Paid ads were rejected, groups were shut down, and an overall mean-spirited nature was abundant in the communities department. Naturally, the adolescent hive-mind downplayed the incident as an imperative to "weed out disinformation".

Around the same time, we also saw the advent of 'Data and Society', what I believe to be a communist think-tank, which involves itself in plans to eradicate influential conservatives from social media. This 'research' group, which is undoubtedly another arm of Mockingbird, is also in bed with Big Tech. If one is to read the list of benefactors, we can see a culture of internationalists, children of eugenicists, communists, judicial representatives, and the crooked media. These include George Soros, Bill and Melinda Gates, The Ford Foundation, Centre for policing equity, Microsoft, UNICEF, Samsung accelerator, Police executive research forum, NYU Information law institute, New York Times, and many more. These are the people responsible for the sudden decline in conservative presence online, through the systematic purging and persecution protocols. Again, this group would not exist today if Trump had not risen to power. It could be implied that the President is indeed the catalyst to bring forth the globalist gauntlet, whereby he is simply controlled opposition. Remember, the globalist modus operandi is to exercise the Hegelian Dialectic; cause and effect. Perhaps, one day we'll find out.

We are living in incredibly scary times. The power Big Tech wields today is unprecedented. No empire in the history of mankind has ever witnessed such an influential weapon to quell dissidents, persecute free thinkers, and control thought, all in the blink of an eye. Our fears have been realised, we are no longer in control of our destiny. After reading the leaked Media Matters manuscript, we can see how Big Tech and Big media have begun their assault on the public.

Google itself has already been caught out by synthetically manipulating search results, of which the corporation eventually confessed doing. By engaging in such practices, the monolith might be publicly judged as being guilty of influencing elections, attempting to overrule the President by aiding others to call for illegitimate impeachment, stifling conservative trends, and boosting detrimental health industries such as big pharma, but the company escapes culpability somehow. Most importantly, the impingement of free speech is now Google's modus operandi, and company policy. Data manipulation and news curation is also the primary objective of the monolith. Type anything about Trump or Christianity, and the search results will always yield negative information, hit pieces, perversion of the Gospel and truth, or completely slanted news. In the top search results, only liberal thought and sources take priority. The rest is buried under twelve inches of liberal crap.

Ironically, Google claims there is no political bias against Trump. But in 2017, Google actually divorced the American President from the phrase "leader of the free world", and substituted it with Angela Merkel's profile instead. This was quite amusing considering how Merkel has systematically destroyed her country by introducing over a million Syrians, many being terrorists. Moreover, Germany is now a hotbed of governmental left-wing fascism and austerity. Naturally, Google's molestation of the truth was textbook Mockingbird style tactics to brainwash the masses into distrusting Trump, and passing the torch to a globalist stooge. One could say that Google's search manipulation was out of sheer pettiness, but it hasn't ended there. Google was also caught deliberately changing algorithms to counter Trump's Muslim ban. Whatever Trump proposed, the system would learn to counter the plan of action with contrary contrived information.

Suddenly, we experienced a search listing blackout on Islamic crimes in Europe, and instead, received only one-sided news on Muslims being persecuted in Burma. Not even the one-time darling of the country, Aung San Suu Kyi, could escape liberal spin and attacks. Within months of Trump's proposed 'Muslim ban', the media and Google became awash with the 2017 Rohingya conflict, while dismissing Syrian migrants who were raping and killing in the EU, en masse. This carried on for around six to ten months, with an incessant bombardment of hit-pieces, charity drives and the typical liberal candlelight vigil. What is most confronting, is that if Rohingyas happened to be Christians, the liberal media wouldn't give them a second look. And no-one can deny this. Without a doubt, Christians are statistically the most persecuted people on the planet. But alas, the media fails to mention that there are roughly around 215 million Christians who are living under oppression, slavery and torture today. But of course, this goes against the liberal narrative. Suffice to say, if Christians were the darlings of the liberal world, their persecution would cease to exist.

From what we've learned after the 2016 election circus, the elites are not entirely afraid of what you say. They're terrified that it can become popular. Without any doubt, social media holds the ability to spread truth to millions throughout all corners of the earth, within a matter of seconds. That is the definition of people power. And that is terrifying to the globalist agenda which is soaked in lies. I would say that the tech giants of today truly had no appreciation for how the tables could be turned on them through their own companies. It's hard to imagine that this has been an egregious oversight for the Marxist overlords, but it is what it is. It's evident that the conservative voice is having the liberal elites running for the hills. They are indeed petrified of us. And censorship is what happens when powerful people get scared.

THE LIBERAL YOUTH INHERIT THE FUTURE

Looking back to 2008, the minute Obama uttered the words "Yes we can", and the ubiquitous "Change", it was clear that the war had already begun. While the gullible masses were baited by the empty promise of a utopia, inspired by a man whom Oprah called 'The One', the echelon had other plans for us plebes. In truth, the words took on a different meaning, and in hindsight, Obama was engaging in double speak. "Yes we can" was the war cry given to his handlers for them to begin the grand operation of pouring communism into every facet of American lives, whether we liked it or not. Indeed, a great deal of 'change' was about to occur, and which would endure for more than eight years.

For nearly a whole decade, near irreparable damage was done to the land of the free, and through Obama's narcissistic pride, no-one would dare challenge him. The America of once was, had slowly became a myth under the fake American's Marxist tutelage. Undeniably, the country's politics and culture had drastically altered to suit a more communist tone. Food stamps and blood donations were at an all time high, as well as welfare pay outs. The economy was literally in shambles, and it was clear that Obama didn't want Americans paying back their mortgages anytime soon. It's evident that he wanted the typical forty year mortgage tied around citizen's necks to malign capitalism, and to present a substitute Marxist financial system to bail out the country. After all, during the global financial crisis, it was Obama whom signed the controversial bank bailout package. It wasn't a loan. It was just giving away free money to negligent firms who were virtually stealing people's life savings and homes. Not surprisingly, we must remember that Obama's cabinet were mostly all appointed by Wall Street.

As the country fell into financial ruin, so did domestic affairs. Terrorist attacks were a monthly occurrence. Black on black crime in Chicago skyrocketed up to four thousand homicides in two years, despite the Black Lives Matter movement in full swing. And all of this happened while the liberal elite grew more powerful through the powertainment culture. They, who we once thought the world of, turned out to be nothing but Marxist shills, blindly following the trend of virtue signalling, and ridiculing middle-America for apparently being poor-mouth, methane producing garbage. And during those hellish eight years, radical Marxist and Islamic groups seemed to pop up everywhere. It was as if the country had begin to tear itself apart. The agenda seemed to fit the Alinsky model of internal destruction, of which Obama praised.

> "Never go to war with an enemy who is killing itself internally."
> - Napoleon

Then came the inevitable liberal infiltration of the internet. Before Obama's influence over the Big Tech industry, the internet itself, and the foremost search engine Google, still bore some semblance of sobriety, balance and transparency of information. Naturally, this drastically changed during the first term of Obama's administration. As mentioned before, his crucial White House meeting with Big Tech helped to consolidate power, and to enact the plan to weed out conservatives, to tip the balance of power forever in the Democrat's favour; or should I say, communists. Likewise, Obama's signing off

ICAAN allowed the tech elite to really corner the internet, and to cut off domains belonging to dissidents. The Marxist plan was all coming together.

Most importantly, freedom of speech was coming under attack for the first time in American history. The communist ghouls didn't do this through conspicuous strong arming, but actually by using the youth to do their dirty work. More than ever, it was our children who worked against us to usher in the socialist utopia they have been indoctrinated to believe in. It is undeniable that today, the youth are the relentless technocrat foot-soldiers who are weeding out dissidents, and ostracising those who don't fit in with their liberal cliques. Of course, this all happened after Mr 'Yes we can' came into power. Historically speaking, the majority vote in the 2008 elections was found to be comprised of mostly young voters. And thus began the ageist society we are living in today, which explains why hardly anyone over the age of forty works in Big Tech.

The world is being run by children. It's a scary thought. Today we are increasingly witnessing the great divide between the youth, and the middle-aged. Those who are unable to keep up with modern tech are shunned as non-progressive, redundant, superfluous and untrendy. So much to the point where grown men are playing video games more than ever to keep up appearances. We can now understand why the average male is becoming ever more juvenile and ignoring the parental instinct. It is during this time we have encountered the term 'man-child', which fits aptly with the current generation of coddled, incapable men. Again, this all happened during Big Tech's infiltration of the family unit, which was overseen by Mr 'Yes we can.'

This hipster, snowflake culture was completely by design. It didn't just spring up overnight. It took years of careful sculpting by Marxist think-tanks to separate the family unit, pacify the nation by feminizing men, and to make both sexes completely unappealing to each other to stop reproduction. Let's face it, what woman really desires a man in his thirties who is obsessed with trends, video games, his bearded, skinny jeaned appearance, and latte drinks? The average woman today secretly desires a burly man, and someone who can protect her, build the family cabin, and wrestle with the bears. Instead, what do we have today? Wimps! It's not a good look, which explains why women are just giving up and following suit. Real men are forthright, dominant, macho, and are born to lead. Today, they're being emasculated by a militant, femme-force of intolerant, precious liberal quasi-lesbians, who are also being taught that "the future is women." They too are repelling men with their half shaved heads, lips full of silicon, the change-up culture, and an overall rejection of maternity. Again, this could not have been achieved without controlled social media to prey on the naive, inherent narcissists who have took the bait, hook, line and sinker. Add rampant abortion in the mix, and you've got what it takes to control society, and depopulate the masses.

There is a specific reason why our society is becoming more ageist, where we shun the elderly as virtual Soylent Green. For those that don't understand this name, go ask your parents. You see, the elderly can impart their wisdom on the youth, and give them comparable evidence to how bad society has become. Let's face it. The world we live in is crap. We're disconnected, paranoid, angry, fearful, narcissistic, and cold-hearted. The former days were nothing like this. People had time for each other, and there was an overall sense of probity in society. Without the elderly to educate our children, it's as if those days never existed. That is the very reason why they're getting rid of granny dearest. She's a liability to the cause. Moreover, the youth today are willing to accept any trendy fascist system, even if it's just Nazism repackaged. Without the grandparents around to warn them of Hitler's historical rise to power, which parallels liberalism today, the fascists have the upper hand. This has only happened since Big Tech arrived on the scene. In a world where your grandparents have no idea how to use the internet, or do online banking, they're as good as dead.

The indolence of the millennial generation, which gives rise to the socialist hand-out culture, have all played into Big Tech's Marxist hands. Silicon Valley, under the guidance of Obama's deep state, has relentlessly preyed on the youth, knowing that they are the future. Like the tech giants today, Hitler himself knew that an ageist society was key in eliminating all resistance. After all, it was the genocidal maniac who once said…

"He alone, who owns the youth, owns the future"
- Hitler

This is why there are more historical photos of Hitler cozying up with the youth, than the elderly. Nonetheless, if the youth today are to inherit the world we live in, God help us all. I cringe to think of what the future holds. Gone are the days where people worked hard all their life to build a legacy for their family. Today's youth are all about the quick and easy buck, overnight successes, where they follow their hipster guru Zuckerberg as *the* moral compass. A man who blatantly stole Facebook, and now controls the world. If our youth can't make it in this world, they blame everyone else but themselves. And this is where the radicalisation begins. We, the hard working people are their enemy, while the elite technocrats support them, by filling their pockets, and brains, with garbage.

Quite disturbingly, the millennial generation today are actually just the offcuts of Obama's former youth brigade. The paramilitary faction which was tantamount to the Hitler youth may now be defunct, but Obama's former henchman project has evolved into none other than ANTIFA. Albeit ineffective, they play a crucial role as the eternal pawn on the game board, who are easily sacrificed. If Hitler were alive today, he would be ever so proud of this rag-tag rabble of indolent no-hopers. For them, their crusade is based on liberal trends, buzzwords, etc. In reality, if one is to ask ANTIFA for what they truly stand for, they actually don't know. It's quite remarkable to see such an organized unit completely speechless over a simple question of purpose. Indeed they are completely braindead, and merely acting on liberal instinct, to hunt and destroy. It's not then surprising that they don't even realise that the tactics they exemplify today, resemble the exact same as the soviets during the Bolshevik revolution. *Down with capitalism! Destroy the family unit! Purge those who disagree with us!*

> "The American people will never knowingly adopt Socialism. But under the name of "liberalism" they will adopt every fragment of the Socialist program, until one day America will be a Socialist nation, without knowing how it happened."
> - Norman Thomas, Former leader of the Socialist Party in the United States, and a six-time candidate for President.

It is the hysterical, mindless, misdirected fervour of ANTIFA and radical liberals which saw Russia fall into a dark era of communism for nearly one hundred years. Today, it's all happening again. This time in the last country renowned for freedom and law. And that is precisely the reason why it is so enticing for the tech elites. America is the last battle.

Undoubtedly, our youth have become more impressionable than ever, and eager to please the cool kids, i.e Google. They have bought into ideals of social unity at the sake of individuality, and are dead-set on homogenizing the world. By using such tools as Facebook, Instagram, Snapchat, it brings the online 'community' together, and binds them tightly. Hitler's vision of a unified world, at the sake of individuality, is identical to the power structure envisioned by Big Tech, which is then passed down to our youth. Hitler's own creed which he forced his people to recite was...

Ein Volk - One people

Ein Reich - One empire

Ein Fuhrer - One leader

As this translates today, liberal progressives are virtually goose-stepping to the beat coming from Silicon Valley...

One people - Liberal progressives

One Empire - A New World Order, or globalism

One leader - Big Tech and the Marxist elite

If you were to tell this to liberals today, they wouldn't listen to you. They are already under a strong delusion, which is irremovable due to their inherent pride. It took the Holocaust to wake the German people up from their spell. I don't foresee it being anything different in the west once Big Tech rules the masses. It's sad to say, that liberal delusion is contagious, but only within their own social circles. And with the current trend of censorship, it's only going to get worse. Today our youth are indeed in a trance, like the Germans were. Like parrots, they mimetically copy trends, speech patterns, lexicons and political thought. For example, there is a new lexicon in the youth culture called 'fam', which is short for family. This truncated word did not come about organically. Somebody planted it in the mind of a brainless fool, who then shared it with their friends, and so on.

The concept stuck like glue, as communism is bound by a community of group-thinkers, all who consider themselves as 'family'. Communism was founded on the precept that all are brothers and sisters. In George Orwell's masterpiece '1984', society refers to each other as brother and sister. This brings about the term 'Big Brother'.

"There is no loyalty but loyalty to the Party. There
is no love except love of Big Brother."
- George Orwell, 1984

The words 'fam', 'bro', 'homey', 'shorty', all signify trust in those who are a part of the system, the millennial generation. With a lack of individuality and self-expression, these are the buzzwords which will ensure that the hive-mind will continue to spread. The youth's impressionable and easily malleable nature also explains the sudden rise of politicised transgenderism, homosexuality, ethnicity, race and women's rights. These issues are nothing more than political cards which the elitist communists have used to divide America for their gain. We must remember, communism might be ultimately about homogenisation for power, but it can only be accomplished through exercising 'divide and conquer'. All empires need a nemesis. And those who fail to embrace what the cultural Marxists are selling, are deemed liabilities.

> "The Communist Party will only be able to fulfil its role if it is organized in a totally centralized fashion, if its iron discipline is as rigorous as that of any army, and if its central organization has sweeping powers, is allowed to exert uncontested authority, and enjoys the unanimous confidence of its members,"
> - Vladimir Lenin

We must remember that before Obama's rise to power, none of these political issues ever received the constant wave of attention that they do today from the media, the education system and the clergy. But in retrospect, the rise of politicised narcism played into the ever-growing problem of political correctness. The tragedy is that Americans believe that the concept was born in America, when nothing could be further from the truth. According to a very old interview with a former KGB agent, which is widely published on Youtube, PC was introduced to the west by communist Russia. It was then embraced by budding new communists in the making such as Hillary Clinton, who predictably focused on race issues to manipulate people. Again, falling into the modus operandi of 'divide and conquer'. This all occurred during the height of the cold war.

In a world gone crazy, one can now cut through the fog of war to see that the Democrats and liberals aren't entirely disorganised and eccentric after all. This monumental shift in politics has culminated from over forty years of community organizing, back alley deals, slush funds, and murder. PC is vital to bring the west to its knees, and it's working splendidly.

> "We shall soon be in a world in which a man may be howled down for saying that two and two make four, in which people will persecute the heresy of calling a triangle a three-sided figure, and hang a man for maddening a mob with the news that grass is green."
> - G. K. Chesterton

Sadly, our own people are cannabalizing for the sake of some alien ideology introduced by ravenous wolves. Those who oppose the system must be destroyed, and at the same time, labelled as 'hateful'. This mentality actually derives from the video game culture of 'zero sum game'. If anyone steps over the line, they must be eliminated.

In keeping with the program of brainwashing our youth with such ideals, we can see that the final step in completely controlling the minds of the masses with fake news and subliminal communist messages, actually goes one step further beyond our current technology. As you read this, the tech elite are desperately trying to push virtual reality on our unsuspecting children. In fact, the draconian and dishonest corporation Facebook acquired the fledgling tech firm Oculus VR in 2014. Oculus was actually financed entirely through crowdfunding, where backers were vehemently opposed to the acquisition with the social media giant. Their fears proved to be well-founded, especially after the data breach scandal in 2018.

Virtual reality looks to become the ultimate tool for the elites. If anyone has seen the photograph of Zuckerberg with the hundreds of drooling participants in Facebook VR auditorium, they would know how scary the concept is. It is through this crucial technology which will blind the user to the world around them, locking them in a liberal-curated ecosystem of Marxist principles. Again, if Hitler were alive today, he wouldn't have needed to invade anybody. He'd simply introduce cheap, poorly made VR headsets to the masses, like Facebook has, and then sell the idea of the 'final solution', neatly wrapped in an algorithm.

It's inevitable that with the video game industry being infiltrated with liberal values, i.e lesbianism, diversity, women empowerment; it's not a stretch to anticipate that the next ten years of gaming tech will introduce even more Marxist ideals. It's only a matter of time before our children will be screaming *"Heil Zuckerberg! Heil Zuckerberg! Heil Zuckerberg!"* In the internal VR ecosystem, where the lines of reality become blurred, we will certainly see our youth emerge as mindless robots all preaching on the 'virtues' of open borders, cultural homogenisation, gender non-binary benefits, followed by the mantra, 'we're stronger together'. Those who resist will be labelled as an extremist, a bigot, a fascist and a Nazi.

With the current state of profile customisation in technology today, it's a guarantee that the socialist brainwashing machine will hinge itself on peak social narcissism, forcing people to take the all natural opiate, self-love. We've noticed over the last twenty years how the media has introduced the concept of loving oneself first before everyone else. Of course, the pretence is apparently to do so out of respect for others. Oprah was one of the first to force this on the masses.

"You can't love others, until you love yourself."
- Oprah

Likewise, cosmetic commercials have all took the bait, displaying on their products the phrase "because you're worth it." You see, there is a reason why this self-love movement came about. Firstly, it keeps people preoccupied with their narcissism, and secondly it prevents external forces besides the state from waking them up. Finally, and by default, if one is not agreeing with you in a homogenized, loving environment, then they must be 'hateful'. It's an ingenious idea, but wholly disturbing. As we have already seen, those who don't fit in with the liberal narrative are immediately classified as 'hateful'. What follows is society, including private companies, shunning said individual until they are no more. For the liberal, the crisis has been averted, their vanity preserved, and the community safe from harm.

Even more disturbing, is that the controlled Marxist press won't investigate why the person was banned, but will virtue signal at the risk of looking like a "fascist" or a "racist". Compliance is safety. Inquiry is questioning the system. As we've learned, the term "racist" now applies to almost anything that goes against the progressive narrative. But again, this wasn't just the result of some retaliating liberal at a loss for words. No, the term 'racist' was devised in the Marxist think tank. Hitler was a master in fabricating new terms to degrade his enemies for political power. These being 'Rats', 'Undesirable', 'Subhuman'. Today, we see the same trend where liberals are calling conservatives 'deplorables', 'dregs of society', 'food eaters.' Socialism always rises to power through the dehumanization of foes. What always follows next is unmentionable, and highly frightening.

> "The idea that you can't use your free speech
> because it is offensive is an idea that… we don't

know if its naivety outdoes its malevolence. Which of those two things are worst? I would go with malevolence, because it attacks something that is absolutely fundamental."

"There are worst things than death. The worst thing than death is hell. And we saw plenty of that in the 20th century. And when we let freedom of speech go, that's where we're headed. And unless we want to go there, then we should stop aiming for it."

- Dr. Jordan Petersen

THE HITLER-LIBERAL ALLIANCE

While the lines between Nazism, Socialism, Marxism and Communism are becoming more blurred within today's context, the rules are quite simple. All of these parties end with the oppression of the people, creation of a small ruling elite, and nationalised, communal control over industry, either through privatisation or corporatism. No person is unique, and no person controls their finances to forge their own destiny without dictatorial government regulation. This is the tech elites plan today. And if we are to look at the world, and how it is developing into a dystopian nightmare, we can see that it is becoming just as Hitler envisioned. Don't believe me? Then I challenge you to refute the following policies of which are identical to liberal progressives. Remember, these weren't penned by the Democrats, but by a man who oversaw the systematic murder of six million people.

Hitler censored people, banned free speech.

The left are hell bent on censoring people who speak the truth and expose their plan. Their ultimate goal is to ban free speech, with the help of Google and Big Tech.

Hitler banned citizens from owning firearms.

The left are attempting to take away all guns and nullify the second amendment. They are doing this slowly through 'gun control' and the demonisation of the arms industry, and social media regulation.

Hitler introduced eugenics, the sterilization of people to stop pregnancies, and was heavily invested in social engineering to make a master race.

The left are already carrying out eugenics, social engineering by mass immigration, and corporately killing off 'deplorables' through Planed Parenthood. P.P was originally created to kill off African Americans, where it was formerly called the Negro Project. The internal policies of this organisation labelled African Americans as 'weeds'.

Hitler empowered women to militancy and control over the 'unter-mensche' or subhuman, a.k.a the deplorables.

The left are heavily invested in exploiting the #metoo movement to empower females to militancy and control in tech-industrial and media sectors; all positions of influence. Today, the cultural paradigm dictates that men are inferior and also irrelevant to women's happiness and security. Left wing groups increasingly hinge their failures on men, by purporting that they, in general, are to blame for the world's problems. The left also consider anyone who opposes them as virtual sub-humans.

Hitler demonized an entire race - the Jews, and anyone who didn't fit in with the Nazi elites' social paradigm, a.k.a the deplorables.

The left emphatically demonise only one race - white people, predominantly males. The current narrative is that white people are the reason for all mankind's problems. When Kanye West supports Trump, they call him a 'white man' as an insult. After meeting President Trump, the left-wing media called it a "minstrel show", dredging up old wounds over segregation. Rapper Snoop Dogg created a picture of Kanye West, depicting the musician as a white man to denigrate him through liberal eyes.

Hitler brainwashed citizens by infiltrating the education system, where he erased the Jews out of German history, calling their existence 'rumour', and stated they suffered with 'Jewish privilege'. He also fabricated a lie that the Germans descended from blonde haired Nordic gods.

The left are re-educating people with socialist values, forcing out conservatism, Christianity, Noah's ark, and creating a cultural vacuum based on class and their assumed biological supremacy, e.g the left vs the 'deplorables'. The new paradigm shift is that white people are inferior, while anyone else must inherit the earth due to their non-white skin colour, and being suppressed by 'white privilege'. There is certainly an element of deification occurring in the liberal circles.

Hitler claimed racial superiority and promoted an ideology of cultural supremacy.

The left have claimed to be superior over conservatives by divorcing themselves from journalistic accountability, and legal culpability over violating the constitution. After the Jussie Smollett scandal, we now know that liberals are not accountable to the law, and simply avoid jail time with their cheque book, or by exploiting their non-white skin colour. They have labelled anyone who opposes them as 'hicks', 'rednecks' and 'deplorables.'

Hitler changed German culture, abolished democracy, and introduced a persecution culture of guilty first until proven innocent.

The left are changing western culture through orientalization. Private left-wing companies are refusing to serve conservatives over "racism" and winning the 2016 election. They also insist on Trump's impeachment despite him not committing an illegal act. The Kavanaugh fiasco proves that the left believe conservatives are not only guilty first before proven innocent, but guilty always until they defect.

Hitler, a socialist, privatised industry, which then was controlled by the government. Only Nazi party members could run businesses of influence.

Google is a socialist, private company with the goal of running the world by proxy through technocratic tyranny. Only liberals are welcome to use the platform through selective elitism. Conservatives are increasingly marginalized.

Hitler changed Germany's religious values and heritage. Hitler hated Christianity, calling it a 'flabby religion' with no merit. He was infatuated with Islam, which provoked him to enlist Bosnian fighters in the SS. Hitler used them as pawns to further his empire.

The left are changing religious values and western heritage, with virtual book-burnings, censorship, historical re-writing, and the removal of important statues. Liberals hate Christianity and slyly twist Bible verses to undermine conservatives. The left is also infatuated with Islam, despite the cult being wholly incompatible with liberal values. Today Muslims are exploited by the liberal elite as pawns in the system, to usher in more security, to further the new world empire.

"The only religion I admire, is Islam."
- Hitler

"The future does not belong to those who slander
the prophet of Islam."
- Obama

THE GOOD CENSOR

Without any doubt, Google has arrogantly taken the role as arbiter of morality and conscience. Even more disturbingly, it somehow believes it has the authority to tell you what is truth and what is false, by discarding information which conflicts with its own principles. The fact that the overwhelming majority of employees at the firm are predominantly leftist, is very unnerving. This would explain the sudden rise in Google's rewriting of history to suit the Marxist narrative. In only the last few years, the company has deliberately altered crucial historical facts to paint leftists as the benchmark of excellence, while undermining conservatives.

For example, Google has been caught red-handed rewriting history by altering President Abraham Lincoln's information bio-section. As it appeared, the details were deliberately changed to 'leader of the National Union Party'. This was completely underhanded, as the N.U.P was a temporary name given to the Republican party, for which Donald Trump is now leader of. Google knows that the Republicans historically fought hard to free the slaves, when in fact it was the Democrats who opposed the emancipation movement. Moreover, it was the KKK who strongly supported the confederate party, and were considered the military arm of the faction. These are the little historical inconveniences that Google is trying to bury.

Moreover, the company has now redefined the term 'fascism', and pinned the definition on the political right, not the left. According to Google, fascism is defined as 'an authoritarian and nationalistic *right-wing* system of government and social organization.' Well, this is simply not true, and more of subjective conclusion than anything. In truth, fascism is described as any system of government which exemplifies strong intolerance to opposing views. It will often use force to remove opponents, and will silence people who disagree with their policies. Does this sound like liberals today? I thought so.

But alas, the rewriting of history at Google's hands isn't out of sheer pettiness. It is just another tactic of their Nazist overlords and handlers. For they know that erasing history is crucial to obtain world power. Without historical context, our youth cannot form an opinion and fight back against the system.

"He who controls the past controls the future. He who controls the present controls the past."
- George Orwell, 1984

Of course, people are starting to wake up to the fact that Google is undoubtedly an Orwellian, Marxist think-tank. American economist George Gilder, aptly criticised the corporation, not only for its recent communist tendencies, but for controlling the minds of people.

"The essence of Google Marxism is that it repeats Marx's error. Marx's greatest error was to imagine that the new inventions of the 19th century, the steam engine, electricity, all of the railroads…had solved the problem of human productivity forever… So in the future, you wouldn't have to worry about creating wealth, you could just focus on distributing wealth."

"Google has even more ambitious statements… they are not just usurping human productivity… They are usurping human minds."
- George Gilder, American economist

Furthermore, psychologist Dr. Robert Epstein also agreed in supporting the fact that Google is now the "most powerful mind-control engine ever created."

"What my research has shown beyond any doubt is that the search engine is the most powerful mind-control machine that's ever been invented in the history of humankind. We are able to shift thinking and opinions and voting preferences and shift thinking about almost anything. We are producing enormous changes in people without them being aware that they are being manipulated."

"Take that another step further and now you have the Google home device which they are trying to get people to put in every room in their house. The Google home device, like Amazon's Alexa, gives you *the* answer to a question. That produces enormous shifts as well in people's thinking and behaviour."
- Dr. Robert Epstein, psychologist

As mentioned, the Google of yesterday pales in comparison to the company it is today. Originally designed to spy on the world via NSA funding, the company did not nearly operate so nefariously as to spy, *and* control the minds of people. We were left alone to think, communicate, and share our ideas. All they wanted was our information. Today, that's not enough. They want the world, and your mind.

"We want to keep the internet open."
- Sergei Brin, Founder of Google

In truth, Google was just a passive analyst, and nothing more. However, sometime after the company met with Obama, something went terribly wrong. Now, the company has evolved to become *the* vanguard against conservative speech, libertarianism, and overall self-expression. If you're not on the liberal train, you're finished.

It's quite disturbing to also discover that suppression of conservative voices isn't just enacted by petty employees, but actually the culture is hinged on internal policies, all manufactured by the top bosses. Only recently a leaked manifesto blew the lid on Google's diabolical practices. Titled 'The Good Censor', the 85 page document outlined Google's long-term plans to virtually kill off anyone who would be deemed a thought criminal. While the document is extensive, I will be brief in summarizing the overall consensus, which was to create an environment of hyper political correctness for 'safety and security'. In other words, pacifying the masses. If they're planning to do this, they must also be expecting a backlash from new dictatorial new world government initiatives about to be unleashed.

The following is a concise summary of what the document prescribes.

Page 2 - The document begins by stating that "users are asking if the openness of the internet should be celebrated after all" and that "free speech has become a social, economic, and political weapon." Like gun control, they must seek to implement speech control.

Page 12 - Staggeringly, it goes on to say the early free-speech ideals of the internet were "utopian," as if global censorship was inevitable.

Page 11 - The document then actually admits that Google, like Twitter and Facebook, practically rule the internet as they "control the majority of online conversations."

Page 15 - The manifesto also mentions Section 230 of the Communications Decency Act, which is crucially tied to Google's position as a platform for free expression. However on page 68, Google now encourages a move towards moderation and censorship as the role of "publisher". This means, as a private company, it grants them the freedom to ban any content which they please.

Pages 19-21 - The document addresses a number of fabricated factors that they believe destroyed faith in free speech. It names the election of Donald Trump and the Russian collusion hoax as predominant reasons. Again, it's possible that Trump is controlled opposition to instigate the leftists in to ushering in censorship. As I mentioned earlier, this is called Hegelian Dialectics.

Pages 26-34 - The document also details how apparent "users behaving badly" undermine free speech. It never explains what is considered 'bad behaviour.' Also the document states that this 'behaviour' on the internet allows "crummy politicians to expand their influence." Most definitely, they're describing Donald Trump. The document also whines that "racists, misogynists, and oppressors" are allowed a voice alongside "revolutionaries, whistleblowers, and campaigners." This alone draws a dangerous line, where Google sees itself as benevolent by default.

Page 45 - Quite shockingly, after the document warns about the rise of online hate speech, it then goes on to hypocritically support the actions of notorious racist Sarah Jeong, through citation. Jeong made headlines for her undoubtedly coached hate speech against white males. Not surprisingly, Google is currently being sued for discriminating against white males.

Page 45 - The document also whines that the internet has become an open platform for freedom of speech, and warns that "rational debate is damaged when authoritative voices and 'have a go' commentators receive equal weighting." This statement is important, as it creates an eternal barrier to protect liberals against criticism.

Page 49 - The briefing then goes on to accuse President Trump of falsely fabricating the "conspiracy theory" that the search engine's autocomplete suggestions showed political bias towards Hillary Clinton during the 2016 election, which is actually true.

Page 54 - Quite surprisingly, despite the document frowning upon "harassment", it then goes on to support the actions of a left-wing social media campaign as a "digital flash mob", comprised of 27,000 members, who are allegedly engaged in "friendly counter-commenting." I mentioned this earlier which was coordinated by the Southern Poverty Law Centre. In other words, a 'flagging' army.

Page 57 - Despite the Russian collusion hoax being exposed, the manifesto then uses a comparison image between Russian election interference and a picture of Donald Trump.

Page 63 - The document also supports the "booting off" of certain groups and individuals from services such as Google, GoDaddy and CloudFlare.

Pages 66-68 - The manifesto then goes on to state that Google, Facebook, YouTube and Twitter are apparently stuck in the middle of two conflicting issues. The first being the "unmediated marketplace of ideas" vs "well-ordered spaces for safety and civility." Google describes the former as a product of the "American tradition" which "prioritizes free speech for democracy, not civility." The latter is then lauded over as a result of the "European tradition," which "favors dignity over liberty and civility over freedom." The document then states Big Tech are now powering forward toward the European tradition. In other words, censorship through political correctness.

Page 70 - The document then has the audacity to use the excuse of a "shift towards censorship" based on alleged regulatory demands, to "protect advertisers from controversial content", and to "expand globally". However, there are no regulatory demands as a publisher, unless the content is illegal. They are free to put whatever content they like. It's just a smoke screen.

Facebook also has followed the same protocols to cut conservatives from the internet. While Google's measures are certainly draconian, I would wager that Zuckerberg's Marxist platform is perhaps worse. In an interview with Project Veritas, a former Facebook employee who wished to remain anonymous, divulged crucial details of the company's cult-like operations. According to the insider, she said...

"Everyone is expected to be the same. At the Facebook orientation, they said the number one rule is 'not to talk about Facebook'. I saw things going on that I personally found to be troubling."

From this interview, we came to learn about programmer Danny Ben David, who was hired to allegedly create algorithms to clamp down on conservative growth. Quite surprisingly, on his website he states…

"I am working at Facebook as a software engineer. I'm part of the problem, I know."

Leaked Facebook documents actually showed a back-end system screenshot of a well known conservative blogger. From what can be seen, Ben David ran a script called "Action Deboost Live Distribution." The insider went on to say that every time she would see the deboost livestream code, Ben David's name was always next to it. As the interview continues, we learn that deboosting is a method of suppressing distribution. For example, it stops people on Facebook from pressing the share button, or using interactive emojis. Also, the live streaming boost button is disabled.

Of course, this is completely Orwellian and downright unethical. But it gets worse. Facebook's A.I is now known to scans videos for certain trigger words; much like how the Stasi listened in on citizens. Through text to speech recognition, the machine learning system identifies 'bad' words that Facebook is against, which the A.I will then trigger the deboosting code. Interestingly, the deboost code is marked next to the algorithmic term "SI", or sigma. This was formerly included to stop suicides or self harm videos. But after 2017, when Trump was elected, the deboost code went political. Further into the interview, the insider says she saw the code appear on many conservatives pages, which explains why the sudden purge of Christian groups and Trump supporters. Most importantly, the insider assured that it had nothing to do with the issue of independent vs mainstream news. Accordingly, there are other independent left-wing accounts on Facebook, but they were untouched.

Other information has come to light which exposes Facebook for designing policies which would make Hitler proud. There is now publicly available documentation which shows that the software engineer and employee, Seiji Yamamoto, worked against conservatives through certain draconian measures. According to records, Yamamoto is a a data science manager for Facebook, where he worked on 'informed sharing ranking demotion' and 'news feed reduction strategy.' On Facebook's private workspace page, he makes it clear he is on a crusade to clamp down on 'hate speech.' However, his definition of hate speech is troubling and ambiguous at best. According to Yamamoto...

"Hate speech needs to be stopped, but there's quite a bit of content near the perimeter of hate speech that we need to address as well."

Project Veritas' insider stated that what this entails is 'things that aren't actually hate speech, but that might offend somebody'. Basically, anything that is perceived as hateful, but no court would define as hate speech. It is from the insider's own private surveillance where she found an internal document called "coordinated trolling on

Facebook", which is tantamount to a 'troll report'. Like Yamamoto, fellow coworker Eduardo Arino de la Rubia was also the author of the program. As records state, this report was to target the meme culture in the past few years. Not surprisingly, due to Facebook's draconian measures, the EU has now put a total ban on memes. It is now criminal for anyone in the Marxist superstate to share such information.

From what Veritas' insider says, we now know that the A.I system targets predominantly conservative words and acronyms like SJW, MSM, and more. The internal system then apparently uses a classifier to weed out people based on suspicion that they're a troll, where certain words are flagged. From the evidence produced, Facebook's internal glossary actually looks like war on words, like deciphering a code. Audaciously, Yamamoto's internal manifesto is eerily similar to Hitler's own psyche-war tactics. The Facebook employee encourages the company to create a system where conservatives, the 'trolls', are to be placed under heavy restrictions to prohibit their activity. However, there is also another primary reason for this…

> "By introducing friction via the troll twilight zone
> will confuse and demoralise them."

As we can see, Facebook is engaging in psychological tactics to control the masses. For example, other evidence which has emerged shows that the system also drastically limits 'offenders' bandwidth for hours, then will auto-logout every few minutes to disorientate. Likewise, the user will also be auto-directed to the home screen timeline every few minutes. Most disturbingly, Facebook looks to wear down non-compliant users where their comments and posts, that they spend time crafting, will magically fail to upload. On top of this, the user will be further logged out again. This psychological tactic is called 'gas-lighting', and has been used in war to make the enemy feel as if they're going crazy.

According to the source, this 'troll twilight control' will be implemented predominantly when leading up to important elections. So in reality, the company is admitting to being involved in election meddling. In a shocking move, Yamamoto also advocates ostracisation through the network by contacting the user's friends over infractions. This is done to warn other potential rebels in the community.

> "When a user does something egregious,
> warranting an account suspension or deletion, we
> should notify the friend network. Fear of being
> outed as a miscreant is what regulates behaviour in
> real life and we should re-introduce that to the
> online world."

In other words, just like the Nazis did with the Jews, those who are seen cavorting with the enemy will be exposed to the public. But of course, Yamamoto doesn't quit while he's ahead, and further engages in psychologic tactics to demoralize his enemies.

> "Notified users who accidentally befriended the
> offender might be more mindful of suspicious
> accounts, increasing overall herd immunity."

It has also been exposed that Facebook now employs what is called a 'troll score index'. Those who are "miscreants", conservatives, authors like myself, are to be deemed as spammers. This is the reason why I have been permanently banned from the platform. What is quite suspicious, is that Facebook doesn't outright declare its political leanings, and hides behind the 'spam' excuse. Project Veritas' insider also states that the problem what the 'troll report' is that it incorporates rapid machine learning. Therefore, when people like myself are booted off the network, there is no recourse or contact department to file a complaint. Of course, this is just the protocol to follow, as the goal is to disenfranchise conservative users, to prevent repeated activity, thus forcing them to conform.

This method of psychological reinforcement has given rise to Facebook's ultimate gaffe which now forces users to 'denounce' content which they share that so happens to be conservative in nature. The move has come as a shock to the online community, which are quickly seeing Facebook for the communist tool that it is. The concept of public denouncement of people, dissidents, and ideas, were all too common in the social uprising in Russia and China.

This is nothing short of social engineering, which is a primary tactic of Marxism. Nonetheless, and not surprisingly, recent news has surfaced that internal memos state Facebook is actively not rewarding 'divisive' content. The company also states they need to promote publishers which are aligned with the mission of Facebook. It's hard to believe that over 2.3 billion people are using the platform today, and are being rigorously brainwashed with curated disinformation. How far this will go, is unknown. But when powerful people become ever more intolerant of their foes, it doesn't take a genius to figure out what comes next when said foe won't go away, or remains an inconvenience.

THEY WHO WANT TO KILL US

It wasn't enough that Hitler and Stalin had crushed their enemies, forcing them into a life of servitude under a brutal regime. They couldn't stop there. Like the mental-illness of obsessive compulsive disorder which is infecting Silicon Valley, despots invariably resort to genocide to eliminate their enemies, once and for all. While the reader may believe this is far-fetched, and that by cutting conservatives from the internet is enough to control the world, I remind that while the Jews in WWII were left to die in ghettos, it still wasn't enough for the Nazis. What followed was a 'final solution' that saw the systematic murder of six million innocent people. After Hitler's 'Mein Kampf' hit the shelves, or what I call Nazi Germany's 'Good censor', the Jews were nominated as the villain in a rising socialist country. They were spat on, called dehumanising names, beaten, and relegated to the gutter. Today, it's all happening again.

Undoubtedly, Big Tech is putting conservatives in the ghetto. Next, through a lack of social credit, trust scores, we will be forced to live a life in the shadow of the uber-elites, which will be virtual death as it is. But I doubt that will be enough. History has proven this. What we are facing is nothing original. If we continue to resist their plans, then they believe that our flesh must be sacrificed for their greater good. If you are to doubt their intentions, then I suggest you read the following quotes by some of the most prominent elites on this planet...

> "I would like to be reincarnated back as a killer
> virus to lower the population."
> - Prince Philip of Windsor

Prince Philip is a super elite 'royal' who has lived off the tax payer for nearly seventy years. His feet never touched the ground. His family were married into the Nazis, and the Queen's uncle was a Nazi who collaborated with Hitler to become a puppet king in a Nazi run empire. Philip also coined the term "food eater" when referring to commoners like you and I.

> "The world's population needs to be decreased by 50%"
> - Henry Kissinger, former Secretary of State

Kissinger has been the forefront in creating a 'new world order', as he puts it. Even during the global financial crisis, where people were losing everything, the man took the opportunity to shamefully shill for his global government.

> "In order to stabilize world population, we must eliminate 350,000 people per day.
> - Jacques Cousteau, Marine biologist

Once beloved for being the adventurous, care-free oceanographer that he was, we now have seen the dark side to Cousteau. Possibly one of the first pioneers to push for the elites' genocidal green deal, his words of extermination are disgusting, as they are shocking.

> "My three main goals would be to reduce human population to about 100 million worldwide"
> - Dave Foreman, Earth First Co-Founder

Another genocidal nutcase pretending to be an environmental conservationist. If systematically killing over 6.9 billion people doesn't send shivers down your back, nothing will. I shudder to think what his other two goals are.

"It's easier to kill 1 million people than control 1 million people."
- Zbiegnew Bejejinski, Polish-American Diplomat and scientist

Spoken like a true Nazi. I'm amazed a Polish descendent would have such flippant regard over human life, considering the Poles own history of persecution under Hitler. Even more disturbingly, this man was a diplomat, and supposed scientist. Not surprisingly, the Nazis were heavily involved in science, to the point where over 300,000 disabled people were exterminated under the Aktion T4 program.

"A total world population of 250-300 million people, a 95% decline from present levels, would be ideal."
- Ted Turner, founder of CNN

When the founder of fake news CNN utters genocidal mantras, is there any wonder why they're losing ratings?

"Childbearing should be a punishable crime against society, unless the parents hold a government license. All potential parents should be required to

use contraceptive chemicals, the government issuing antidotes to citizens chosen for childbearing."
- David Brower, first Executive Director of the Sierra Club

It's understandable now why the left are dead-set on supporting Planned Parenthood. Included in the Democrats green deal, questions over whether to allow couples to have children have been raised. It's evident that the genocide has begun, and anyone who stands in their way must also be exterminated.

"A program of sterilizing women after their second or third child, despite the relatively greater difficulty of the operation than vasectomy, might be easier to implement than trying to sterilize men. The development of a long-term sterilizing capsule that could be implanted under the skin and removed when pregnancy is desired opens additional possibilities for coercive fertility control. The capsule could be implanted at puberty and might be removable, with official permission, for a limited number of births."
- Barack Obama's top science advisor, John P. Holdren

It's hard to believe that such people have been staffed in the White House. These policies are the exact same communist birth protocols that were introduced in China over thirty years ago. History tends to gloss over what happened to Chinese nationals who broke the rules.

Like today, forced abortions and sterilisations were not uncommon. Reported stories of babies being ripped from the womb, and thrown into the bin, are abundant. Like China, federal states are pushing for abortions at full-term, and killing the child after delivery. I guess Obama's policies never left the hill when Trump came into office, after all.

> "Birth control must lead ultimately to a cleaner race."
> - Planned Parenthood Founder Margaret Sanger.
> Woman, Morality, and Birth Control. New York:
> New York Publishing Company, 1922. Page 12

Indeed, what the public is unaware of, through censorship of course, is that Planned Parenthood was designed to exterminate predominantly African-Americans. Disgustingly, the organisation actually had the audacity to refer to black people as "weeds."

> "Frankly I had thought that at the time Roe was decided, there was concern about population growth and particularly growth in populations that we don't want to have too many of."
> - U.S. Supreme Court Justice Ruth Bader Ginsburg, on Roe v Wade 'The case which legalised abortions.'

Of course, Ginsberg is referring to African-Americans, as Planned Parenthood was initially targeting them. It's astonishing today to see the left-wing media and Hollywood lauding over this woman, making flattering movies about her. In reality, the woman is nothing but a white-supremacist, genocidal thug who hates black people. It's hard to believe a Jew would support the systematic murder of a race. But here it is in black and white, no pun intended.

> "This year, the United States renewed funding of reproductive healthcare through the United Nations Population Fund, and more funding is on the way. The U.S. Congress recently appropriated more than $648 million in foreign assistance to family planning and reproductive health programs worldwide. That's the largest allocation in more than a decade – since we last had a Democratic president, I might add."
> - Hillary Clinton

From what we can see, Clinton certainly has been cooking the books to usher in a global genocide program to depopulate the planet. Eerily, she makes the contribution that 'more funding is on the way', no doubt at the expense of the unsuspecting American tax payer. And just to think, the US almost had this woman as President.

> "What would it take to accelerate fertility decline in the least developed countries?"
> - The March 2009 U.N. Population Division policy brief

The U.N has a history of doing nothing to stop regional genocide throughout Africa. In fact, founder of Microsoft, Bill Gates, is working closely with the proxy world order by using vaccines to kill off Africans. This is a proven fact, and not speculation. The Kenyan Catholic Doctors Association say that they have uncovered evidence of a mass sterilization program sponsored by the government and funded by Bill Gates' 'charity'. Rumours have also persisted, although denied by liberals, that Gates won't get his children vaccinated. I wouldn't be surprised. Moreover, it's important to mention that Gates' father was rumoured to be attached to the 'Cold Spring Harbor Laboratory', which was dedicated to eugenics. It is from that institution, where Gates's father, and he alike, worked with Planned Parenthood.

"The U.N can and should play an essential role in helping the world find a satisfactory way of stabilising world population…"

"We are on the verge of a global transformation. All we need is the right major crisis, and the nations will accept the New World Order."
- David Rockefeller, Internationalist and bankster, U.N Dinner, 1994

Well Dave, the Nazis sure found a way to stabilise the population… by building death camps. Like I already mentioned in this book, Rockerfeller just gives away the game by stating that chaos precedes order. What crisis he's talking about, we'll never know. But I hope it never happens.

"(About conservatives) They're a small percentage
of the American people… Some of them the dregs
of society."
- Joe Biden, Former vice president and presidential
candidate

I suppose when presidential candidates think of conservatives with such regard, it's easy for them to enact a plan of genocide. Indeed, at one time the Jews were also a small percentage of the German people, and Hitler also referred to them as the dregs of society. Look how that ended.

"(On conservatives) No, no… When they go low, we
kick 'em. That's what this new Democratic Party is
about."
- Eric Holder, former attorney general

Interestingly, Holder's call for 'action' against conservatives sounds eerily like how Hitler's Brown shirts came into power. But this is typical of a party who has nothing to offer the people, and so desperately desires to rule the world.

"You know, to just be grossly generalistic, you could
put half of Trump's supporters into what I call the
basket of deplorables."
- Hillary Clinton, former secretary of state and
presidential candidate

There it is folks. The undeniable truth that one day, our heads will be on the chopping, for the 'greater good'. What gives these people the right to exterminate anybody indiscriminately? Who died and made them king? When the liberals speak of Hitler, they rightly condemn him for genocide. But when the U.N, globalist elite, Hollywood and our own politicians call for 'destabilizing the population', they sycophantically laud each other, and praise the notion as virtue.

If this is our future, we're already doomed.

OUR BLEAK FUTURE

When I think about the near future, and the world our children will live in, I literally shudder. A cold sweat passes over my body, and I am confronted with the realisation that we are losing the west to a demonic underbelly, a shadow government, who are unapologetically using Muslims and Islam as the battering ram to bring us all down. It wasn't by accident that over one million Syrian Muslims flooded into the EU. It wasn't by accident that our police service would not act upon Muslim rape gangs, but instead preferred to paint their nails with the rainbow motif and chase down 'thought criminals'. It wasn't by accident that our politicians have all failed us, seeming more interested in protecting the feelings of criminals, terrorists, pedophiles and rapists. It wasn't by accident that the west suddenly embraced the term 'political correctness', giving way to a deluge of stifling 'hate speech' laws. No. This was all by design.

For a *selectorate* elite who apparently possess the highest form of intellect in our civilization, they're pretty stupid. Why would anyone want to destroy their own country and replicate the same standards that refugees have fled from? The answer lies in Marxist indoctrination, which is paving the way for the thousand year plan called the 'New World Order.' The elites have all bought into the scam that one day, they and their kin will rule in a perpetually dynastic, totalitarian society, where the rule of law is made by them, to serve only them, and to subdue the masses for their will. It is evident that they believe by perverting democracy with election rigging, hoax political witch-hunts and disenfranchising the voter base, people will naturally embrace the alternative option by default through indifference or desperation for order - communism. This is the world we are speeding towards, and the Marxist beast is not slowing down anytime soon. The west was once a well-oiled machine with an overall sense of probity that encouraged honestly gained prosperity, the pursuit of happiness, and the freedom to not only speak, but to think. Today, that reality is quickly vanishing. Our ideals have become compromised, our culture has become toxic. Humour is now a sin, and rationalism is for those considered eccentric, or outright insane. In all, the world is slowly falling into chaos. But as what is written on the American dollar bill, *Annuit Coeptis Novus Ordo Seclorum* or "Our New World Order is Crowned with Success", it gives perspective to the latin term *Ordo ab chao*, or "Order out of chaos."

To give our dystopian society some frame of reference, we must cast our memory back to the infamous, milestone speech given by George Bush Snr.

> "What is at stake is more than one small country, it is a **big idea** — a **new world order** where **diverse** nations are drawn together in **common cause** to achieve the **universal** aspirations of mankind: **peace and security**, freedom and the rule of law."
> George Bush Snr - **September 11**, 1990

It is from this virtual declaration of war on humanity, that we can now understand that we have all been played as pawns in a sick game of world domination. Bush's ominous speech gives us an insight into why our governments have suddenly become obsessed with 'diversity', and the ubiquitous term, 'common purpose'. The only liability to their

154

cause is truth, reasoning and patriotism. It is because of this that global censorship is now state policy, enforced not entirely by the state, but by corporations; companies acting as the de facto arm of a worldwide shadow government. For them, the truth must be suppressed at all costs, lest it give away the game.

A great deal is at stake for the elites. The sun is slowly setting on the old ways, and a 'change' is coming, ushering what they call the 'new age'. Trillions of dollars have been spent over the last forty years towards nation building, pseudo-democratic colonialism, and economic, political manipulation, all to serve the great cause. This has not been achieved through democratic means, but facilitated only through media manipulation, constant wars, and most importantly censorship, all deriving from cultural Marxism; the sneaking cancer which has infested our civilization. And if we take a quick peek into the west, we can see that their plan is coming into full fruition.

OVERRULED BRITANNIA

What has become of the great west? More importantly, Britain, one of the earliest pioneers of free expression, liberty and justice. The iconic song *Rule Britannia*, penned by Thomas Arne is a distant reminder to what the country actually once was.

> "Rule, Britannia! Britannia, rule the waves!
> Britons never, never, never shall be slaves.
> The nations not so blest as thee
> Must in their turn, to tyrants fall.
> While thou shalt flourish great and free:

The dread and envy of them all."

Britain. Today, a nesting ground for the corrupt establishment, a feckless, bloated monarchy, and a pacified nation, who are most certainly slaves. Indeed, at one time Britain was blessed as the song states. The tiny country that stood up to tyranny, the Nazis. It used to be the envy of all, and to be feared, through the power of the people. It lead the abolition of slavery, and was the antithesis of fascism. It is the resting place of Churchill, Elizabeth the great and anti-slavery advocate, William Wilberforce. Through a steady decline of over forty years, it is a shadow of its former self. And there is a good reason why this is so.

It might appear to be insignificant today, but what is crucial is that the UK is the linchpin in the Marxist empire about to be formed. Despite being a quisling state to the EU, weird, and unbalanced in its logic, Britain is still a world leader in cultural change and development. Despite its crumbling infrastructure, it is a crucial landmark for being the last ostensible remnant of an independent empire which controlled a thriving democratic commonwealth. While the commonwealth may be loosely glued together, the fabric is slowly coming apart. We can already see the signs of Great Britain's secession from independence, and its over reliance on the monolithic, totalitarian superstate known as the EU, the political neo-empire which was created by Hitler in 1941. Ever since the UK officially signed the treaty of Lisbon, we have seen the worst occurring in once was such a green and pleasant land. When I say that the UK is now under the control of Marxists, and Nazi's in tweed suits, I do not speak in jest. For what it's worth, the government may as well run the swastika up the flagpole, considering the royal family's sordid past with uncle Hitler.

The UK is no longer free. The pure spectacle of histrionics in Westminster over Brexit, and its defiance to honour the people's vote speaks volumes. The days of Cromwell, the Magna Carta, speaker's corner and jolly ol' England are over. The local 'bobby' or policeman is no longer your friend. He's the bureaucratic thug who's made it clear that the state 'security' department, or Stasi, are watching your every move online, just waiting for any excuse to arrest you for 'hate speech.' And if it isn't creepy enough that your local town centre is infested with CCTV, the government has now installed microphones on lamp posts to listen on conversations. If you think these are the limits to Britain's Orwellian dictatorship, think again.

Anyone who is seen flying an American and British flag together outside of Buckingham palace has to be escorted to a 'public' area. Apparently, the royal family now vehemently objects to the sacred American-British alliance, which is being dismantled by the Marxists in British government. After all, who cares if both countries have been the strongest allies for over a hundred years. Those days are finished. It seems today that the British government and royal family are far too concerned with keeping up with Twitter trends and liberal manners, then looking after their own people. Therefore, I do not believe that it's unfeasible that we will soon see monarch to be, Prince Charles, cutting the ribbon at the local mosque, or perhaps attending the opening of the coming supreme London Sharia court. After all, Charlie wants to be the 'defender of all faiths', despite being the sole appointed head of the Church of England.

But who could blame him considering that five years ago, British law permitted the peaceful protest of any mosque development, whereas today it is now a crime punishable with jail, as it constitutes a 'racial' offence. Of course, this wouldn't have anything to do with

Charles' prior visit to the Saudi states, where he was seen dressed up like Laurence of Arabia, dancing with sword in hand. There is nothing more shameful than seeing a future monarch selling out, especially in such poor attire. But this is the climate our Marxist government has fostered. The Queen and her family are just ornaments in an ever increasing communistic British Isles, where her ilk are forced to virtue signal and begrudgingly feign interest in the 'food eaters', as Prince Philip calls us. We all remember the rotten spectacle the nation saw when the Queen was made to grovel and do penance for the Grenfell tower fire; an incident that became more political than tragic. To say that the British establishment has become more obsessed with minorities, Islam, and keeping up appearances than rebuilding churches, preserving our liberties and maintaining their sovereignty, is an understatement. This would never have happened thirty years ago. The Queen would not stoop so low as to pander to a political wildcard, more so with such low security detail. This is the state of the UK in 2019, and it's only occurred since communism infiltrated Westminster.

They've all sold out. Somehow, it's apparently culturally acceptable to let in a few thousand terrorists, all returned from the homicidal summer camp called ISIS. According to British parliament, these unfortunate souls need to be 'deradicalized' instead of being tried for treason and crimes against humanity. Of course, this is understandable in context when Wills and Kate were seen cavorting with the Obama's in Buckingham palace, like it was just another Sunday cook out. Obama, the man who created the terrorist vacuum in the middle-east, whose feet was up on the royals' couch, surely couldn't have anything to do with the sudden decline in probity in the UK. Could he? Where has Britain's common sense gone when our elected politicians fawn over murderers, but persecute liberty activists and academics who desire to enter the country to engage in open debate? In a nation gone mad and in the process of slow suicide, I suppose it is not shocking to witness the education system encouraging children to adopt Islamic names for a day, and forcing mosque attendance to learn the finer things about Islam. You know, jihad, apartheid, the cornerstone of the faith. Of course, if the parent protests, trouble awaits. Reports have documented that children are now more likely to bully non-attendees for being racist and bigots. If you don't believe me, do your own research.

To add insult to injury, the education system is now refraining from teaching children about the holocaust, lest it upset migrant students, which goes to show what kind of migrants are entering the country en masse. A recent study showed that schools are rapidly filling up with Muslims from all corners of the world, leaving the local albino Brit as the minority. According to news sources, Muslim parents have threatened and bullied local schools into removing this crucial historical event from the books. Further developments have also been documented which show that local 'white' children are being bullied and assaulted for apparently being 'Christian'. God help the child if he's Jewish. Has the government stepped in to curb this issue? Not a chance.

I suppose it's not surprising considering that the government and police have idly stood by while Muslims have for years antagonised the public by waving placards with writings such as 'the real holocaust is coming', and 'Allah bless Hitler.' Indeed, the holocaust is destined to happen again through the education system's failure to teach children on the horrors of political persecution, and the abolition of free speech. But where is Nigel Farage, former leader of UKIP in the midst of all this? At one time, the man was tipped to become the defender of the Christian faith, and a great restorer of British culture. To quote the man...

> "On the question of Islamification, I think we have to do a bit more, probably starting in our schools, to actually teach people of the values of our Judeo-Christian culture... because I'm getting a bit tired of my kids coming home from school being taught about every other religion in the world, celebrating every other religious holiday, but not actually taught about Christianity. There are now twenty police forces in this country that turn a complete blind eye to the operation of Sharia courts and Sharia law. If you're not prepared as a nation, from the top down, to stand up for your culture and your values, then those cultures and values will be threatened."

Unfortunately, that's all changed. Today, Farage has distanced himself from his former days of acerbic, meaningful rhetoric. Instead, he's betrayed his party, formed his own 'culturally acceptable' vanilla junket, accepted millions of pounds in donations, maligned his former comrades and hypocritically u-turned on the issue of Islam. It seems the man has become just another talking head in a sea of insipid communists, who are all too afraid to say it truthfully. To be frank, the man is a shill and a closet Europhile. He talked the talk, but didn't walk the walk. The irony is that he denounced Tommy Robinson as a racist, despite the quoted speech being completely identical to T.R's own manifesto. To top it off, Farage despicably referred to supporters of UKIP as a 'loutish fringe', or perhaps 'food eaters' as the royals call them. These 'louts' are the people who gave their hard earned money to the party, while Farage ran off to Brussels and got paid $500 a day for speaking what in retrospect appears to be pompous, hollow platitudes. Most interestingly, this is a man who has said that he wants to abolish the two party political system, which by default would mean only one dominant party. To me, this sounds like a dictatorship. I suppose it's too late to rely on Nigel to back free speech. After all, if he did, he would be supporting Tommy Robinson's right to free assembly, regardless if he's a 'racist'. Chance would be a fine thing.

EUROMEGALOMANIA

If we were to look back at the UK fifteen years ago, it was completely unrecognisable, and in a good way. What the British Isles is facing today is a cultural revolution, a takeover by foreign powers, undoubtedly coming from communist China, whom both the UK's and the EU's hands are firmly in Shanghai's pockets. The careful, and coordinated destruction of Britannia could only have happened through state-run BBC communist propaganda, the Islamic infiltration of the education system, and the total and complete abolition of free speech to combat 'Islamophobia'. Islam is indeed the battering ram to bring the west to its knees. The British communists in power are relishing every moment, and are eager to report back daily to their EU overlords.

This is what the UK has become. A sinking ship which plays on the fabricated term, Islamophobia, to ultimately weaponise 'hate speech', to completely destroy free speech. Of course, this is all steeped in Hegelian Dialectics. A concept which supports subversive action to combat negative consequences. We can understand now why the UK has become a quisling country which shuns liberty, and imprisons heroes such as Julian Assange. The man who risked it all, only to be humiliated and lifted off his feet to perhaps the *worst* maximum security prison in the UK, all on trumped up charges. But alas, this great purge we are witnessing is to usher in non-pluralistic, monotonous thought. And it's all to align with the EU's draconian standards.

With the EU's mandated plan to bring in over 50 million Muslim migrants within less than a decade, it can only mean disaster for the continent. With the overwhelming burden of supporting over one million Muslim Syrians migrating to Germany and Scandinavia, we have witnessed the worst behaviour of mankind since the Nazis marched through Europe. Each day that passes, the European media struggles to suppress the truth about rising rape gangs in Sweden, Finland, Germany and the Netherlands. No-go zones are now a fact of life in the EU, where the local municipality no longer has control over their cities. Stabbings, acid attacks, rape, racketeering, hijackings, theft, pedophilia and murder are happening at an unprecedented rate, all at the hands of Muslim immigrants. And as the indigenous remain helpless, due to the police refusing to investigate at the risk of being labelled 'racist', the EU bureaucrats continue to pander to the trouble-makers ostensibly for votes.

It's a horrible state of affairs when the elderly are being forced to relocate from their lifelong homes to make way for terrorists and gangsters, and yet, nobody is there to help them, or stop the madness that is pouring out from Brussels. But again, this steady destruction of the EU is orchestrated, and hasn't been left to chance. Again, falling back into the Hegelian Dialectic syndrome, where jihad creates more security, and exponentially increasing Muslim crime introduces a police state. From 'order out of chaos', we will see the world map change irrevocably.

In truth, Europe is finished. The remnant of western democracy and Christian ideals have no more than ten years left on that continent. What will soon follow is an Orwellian police state, where the rule of law protects only the elite, and for a short while, Muslims, until Islam is outlawed under state policy. After all, religion cannot exist in a communist empire. Only the supreme leader shall exalt himself as god in the holy of holies. Nonetheless, Islam still has much use for the globalist elites. More so in silencing the masses. Already, in the EU it is now a criminal offence to critique the religion. Not criticise, but simply critique. Thus to do so is a 'hateful' act. And as we can see, the intrinsic link between 'hate' and mental illness is slowly being pushed through the media. One can't truly appreciate how dangerous the term 'hate' has become. It's not enough to segregate society, but to usher in protocols to re-educate hateful people, i.e those who resist the new world order. We've already seen this exemplified with right-wing French politician Marine Le Pen, whose presidential dreams were shattered by obvious election rigging and demonization. While the public may not be aware, Le Pen did not just quietly fade away into the night. She was immediately, and ruthlessly persecuted for uploading a critical picture of ISIS, whereby the French state then ordered her to complete a psyche exam. A humiliating tactic to debase, and break the will of an opponent, through public ridicule, and gaslighting her by implying that she was suffering with a mental illness. This is protocol in communist countries, of which France has become. Those who are refusing to comply and go with the flow, are considered crazy and must either be re-educated or imprisoned.

In Germany, the trend of forced indoctrination is also palpable. Reports have also documented citizens being terrorised by state police for uploading content which criticises Islam. But it doesn't stop there. These citizens are then forced to attend weekend courses, where they are, to put it bluntly, brainwashed into accepting Islam. If they still fail to comply, they are threatened with financial ruin and prison. This cult style form of bullying is what the EU has become today, and it's only going to get worse. Even in the UK, the term 'mental illness' has already been weaponized for many years, under the state term 'sectioning'. While the media is not reporting this phenomena, hundreds of innocent people, all victim of the system, have already been threatened with the black mark lest they lose custody of their children. Like the term 'hate', we still can't truly appreciate the extent of how the elites will exploit this situation. While one may deduce that both hate and mental illness are synonymous, the truth is that a 'hateful' person in the USA can still purchase a firearm to protect themselves, and the constitution. A 'mentally ill' person however is a whole different issue. We can now understand why there has been a sudden rise in journalist coverage on 'depression' in society and famous 'suicide' stories. Moreover, when mass shootings have been somehow allegedly linked to 'mental illness'. Most are indeed the product of, but not all. Still, mental illness is slowly becoming an umbrella term which encompasses all behaviour which defies the state. And it's through 'mental illness' how they'll enact gun-control.

THEY WILL BREAK YOU

To slowly break the will of the people, the new communist state must destroy the former culture, its religion and sovereignty. While this systematic approach to overthrowing democracy has been occurring for some years, the ultimate act of betrayal and subjugation has come through the Notre Dame cathedral burning. Plans to rebuild the destroyed cathedral are already been designed which will audaciously incorporate Islamic minarets into the structure on the pretence of appeasing the local liberal and Muslim populous. I am not kidding. Do your own research. The truth is that this was orchestrated to divert the attention from the growing yellow vest rebellion, and to bring France further to its knees by erasing its heritage. This is textbook Marxism, of which we saw happening in China in the 1950s, where Mao converted houses of worship into government sanctioned buildings. Of course, the trend of converting churches into mosques is nothing new. The amount of churches in the UK that have fallen to Islamic control is staggering.

When the UK and EU fall to the hands of totalitarian one-percenters, how long will it be until America, the land of the free, buckles under pressure to conform? It's not a matter of when. It's happening as you read this. Socialism is gripping the republic, forcing people to conform through sly tactics such as social shaming, doxing, character assassinations, phoney calls of racism, historical muckraking and even more depraved acts. While this trend continues on the surface, the deep-rooted Islamic cultural invasion is occurring throughout the country, all at the behest of the Marxist establishment. Islamic terror camps are already being discovered in parts of the country such as Alabama. But of course, through jihad comes more state security. Like the UK, it is inevitable that the USA will face the same fate through slow Islamization in urban areas, forcing conservatives out of the main power hubs. Detroit, Michigan and now Minneapolis are already a hotbed of terrorism, no-go zones, and Islamic enclaves. Not surprisingly, America's cousin to the north, Canada, is also having immense problems with Islamic infiltration, only just a few miles over the US border. Therefore there's no guessing why the first Muslim congresswoman Ilan Omar, hailing from Minnesota, is already dividing the nation and burrowing deep into American politics with her Hamas-aligned, radical Islamic views.

It doesn't take a genius to figure out that within ten years, the north mid-west region will begin to implode through sectarian squabbles and conflict over US legislation and Sharia law. Indeed, the American constitution is already in crisis, with the majority of the bill of rights quickly becoming redundant. The sneering, callous cabal in DC referred to as the mysterious 'deep state' are doing everything they can to keep up with Britain's already 'progressive' system of persecution and control, by using useful idiots such as radical Muslims and former hippies as their foot-soldiers. Had Trump not won the election, who knows how far down the rabbit hole Hillary and her henchmen would have taken America. Even with the high witch of DC out of office, it is still heartbreaking to see the land that gave us the immutable first amendment, the basic right of any human which was protected universally through the once free internet, now under attack by her ilk. Long gone is the era of free and open discussion without fear of persecution. Our world has become one where the cornerstone of liberal free speech is deceit, subterfuge and gaslighting. Truth itself has become the antiserum against the great liberal lie. And we're running out of chances to inoculate the innocent against the rising tide of looney lefties, all on the war path to malign and trample their opposition.

Liberals absolutely abhor the truth. Indeed, 'truth is the new hate speech', for no liberal can turn illogic into common sense. Nothing could be truer in this day and age. The term 'hate' is now fully realised as a political broadsword, where the weapon is being used throughout every sector in our society. Most importantly, the new power card has been embraced with open arms by our youth, who have been indoctrinated to believe that it is trendy to shun the 'hateful', 'bigots', 'racists', while rewarding compliance and dogmatic obedience. It is clear that the youth of today have been rigorously brainwashed by the China-state infiltrated media, communist liberal professors, braindead celebrities and their own ilk to excessively virtue signal, by exploiting every minority, sexuality, gender and non-white race for political gain. This is the first preliminary tactic of communists which is always witnessed before a great cultural revolution, where genocide (ethnic cleansing) then quickly follows. As I already mentioned, this practice is called 'divide and conquer'. The rising radical state deems what is good, and what is to be hated. It draws a line, forcing all to comply at the risk of being targeted for persecution. With Germany in the 1930s, it was the Jews. In the 1970s Cambodia, it was the academics. China's revolution began in the 1960s, by purging the nationalists. Russia in the early 1900s, it was the imperialists. In the west, circa 2018, it's the conservatives, Christians, caucasians, nationalists, and the working class. History always repeats with communism, for they can only fall back on old dirty tricks, and repackage them to be disguised as western progressivism.

At present, liberals are exploiting transexuals for political gain, but tomorrow, it is whatever useful and dispensable pawn they can use.

They've tried the Boycott Israel (BDS) movement, Black Lives Matter, Planned Parenthood, #metoo, and any other fickle cause the social justice warrior can put its hand on. They don't really care about the plight of people. In truth, it's a smokescreen. Narcissists can only care about themselves. But much like psychopaths, they will continue unabated. Even if it means targeting a woman for saying 'have a gay day' to a disgruntled thug in a carpark, they'll milk the situation until they seize the ultimate power card. Tomorrow, it's a child being called racist for eating a 'brown' chocolate easter bunny. The next day, it's the vilification of 'white' milk as a conspiracy over white supremacy. If you think this is far-fetched, then I suggest you do your own research to see how far communist liberalism has flushed us down the toilet. In parts of the west, it is now a criminal offence to misgender someone by accident, or to publicly state that there are only two genders. With societal standards as ours, I bet the future generation is going to be so disturbed and confused, that they won't know an anus from a vagina. This is your destiny in the making. And to think, that these people are going to be the next leaders who will appoint even more feckless and idiotic cohorts to watch over you when you're old and grey.

RULED BY FOOLS

All of this lunacy has been fuelled by communist-designed social media networks, where young liberal minds are trapped in an ever-shrinking echo chamber, filled with confirmation bias and rancour. This is why the weak-minded fools scream, 'resist! resist! impeach! impeach!' Those who conform are rewarded with social credit points known as 'subscribers', 'followers', virtual pats on the back, without the fear of community strikes to take down their precious social pages. Display the rainbow flag on your profile picture, the mark of the beast, and you're immune to the purge. Place a Christian cross on your page, and Muslim foot-soldiers will complain that it's offensive to their beliefs, to have your account removed. This is slowly becoming the norm, where sanity is slowly losing its voice. The age of orchestrated narcissism celebrated its coming of age with the advent of Facebook and Twitter, both being platforms designed not only to spy like a communist network, but to reinforce the Marxist ideals of group think. In communist China, the revolution was fomented and ultimately controlled by the 'gang of four', Mao being the supreme leader. Today, we have a new gang of four. Facebook, Google, Youtube and Twitter. A despotic collective of technocratic cult members, and latte sipping, megalomaniacs. If Mao was alive today, he would be salivating over the prospects of a worldwide spy system, fully integrated throughout a global telecommunication platform, all neatly packaged in the guise of a happy clappy, commie social club. Not even he, Marx, Lenin or Stalin could come up with such a diabolical plan. Today, social media's communistic roots lie in the concept of synergetic brain networking, or hive-mind reasoning. This structure is actually modelled on China's 'Project Dragonfly', a social network designed exclusively by Google, solely for China, where citizens are permanently spied on and rewarded for ratting out dissidents for social credit. Those who refuse to take the social mark of conformity, may not buy nor sell. Period.

We can now understand why millennials are becoming more and more like the Hitler youth, and little Maos in the making, day by day. As I previously mentioned, it's all accomplished by tapping into their inherent narcissism. As our youth are repetitiously encouraged to love themselves more than others, the problem gets worse, and we begin to lose our sovereignty, dignity and future. It's hard for a liberal to look at the world for what it is, when they spend more time looking at themselves in the mirror. In a world of self-love, it is understandable why our precious youth have turned into the most sensitive people in the world, and are unable to take criticism or alternative views. But don't let the facade fool you. They might appear to be 'snowflakes', but without any doubt, our youth have become the nastiest, vicious and vilest people in modern history. As the saying goes, 'they can give it out, but they can't take it.' And again, the term 'hate' is the ultimate liberal trump card. If you don't agree, you're hateful. If you have a better argument, or the liberal cannot answer back, you're hateful. 'Conform or die' will be the new maxim written on every street corner within only a few years to come. They're already saying this albeit through their forked tongues, and under the guise of smarmy political correctness and passive aggression. And it's our youth today who are inheriting this cultural normalisation of fascism. These are the people Lenin referred to as 'useful idiots'. Idiotic, and useful to Karl Marx, they most certainly are. It is from their community organizing, pioneered by radical leftists like Obama, where the indoctrination spreads. You see, our youth no longer sees the world as the layman does. They are in a cult, and for them, it is all or nothing. We, the unimportant, and un-enlightened, are merely expendable.

With a dangerous mindset like so, it explains why congresswoman Alexandria Ocassio Cortez' green deal sounds more like the Nazi party's 'final solution'. To them, we are just useless, ignorant 'food eaters', 'climate change deniers', 'methane producers', who are beneath them. A rag tag bunch of 'deplorables', or 'the dregs of society' as presidential hopeful Joe Biden calls us. We're just simply not worthy of living. We have no future in the communist 'paradise' they are so close to establishing. Thus, we can understand the pure hatred regularly caught on camera when liberals viciously attack anyone who fails to conform. These brainwashed youth have been trained through the teachings of Alinsky Marxist proteges, and liberal social media, to shout down at anyone who dare defy them. We've all seen the footage of Democrat adolescents caught spitting, punching and swearing at conservatives. These non-isolated tirades can only be described as deriving from some form of mental illness, but it is they who call the God-fearing as 'crazy'. Not surprisingly, liberal's irrational and desperate fervour was witnessed in both early Nazi Germany with the Brown shirts, Hitler youth, and during the Chinese cultural revolution. Like today, where fired-up liberal youth have been witnessed smashing historical statues in the name of social justice and 'racism', the Chinese communists and Nazis alike also implored citizens to burn, destroy and erase every shred of their history through book-burning, art defacement, and terrorism. Indeed, the cultural revolution of the west is here, and it will continue unabated.

But alas, our commie-infiltrated education system is careful not to teach the ignorant of these historical events, lest they recognise the parallels in their own culture. It is therefore no surprise why our schools are more interested in focusing on identity politics, and a feel-good, vapid syllabus. This is the grand distraction. The end goal is to deter our youth from learning about real freedom, not just some cultural trend steeped in Marxism. It is thus for obvious reasons why our education system is failing to teach children about the bill of rights; the precious article penned by forefathers who knew that this horrid day would come. Alas, the government's failure to instil that perpetual mentality of emancipation from political tyranny is of course by design. For obvious reasons, they're not teaching children their natural

God-given rights in school because it's easy to take them away if they don't even know what they are, or if they exist. It's like a game and not knowing the rules. Thus, the opposition has the upper hand, and the status-quo appears to be so. When I use the term opposition, I mean the government. We used to be able to depend on duly elected representatives, in some respect, but not anymore. We're slowly being put through the meat grinder, and they're smiling all the way.

To make matters worse, the world we live in is no longer guided by a noble, honourable, wise patriarchy, but a snivelling, juvenile tech elite. An overprivileged, brain-dead, bunch of keyboard warrior billionaires, not any older than thirty-five. It's a sad fact, but the overlords we are cowering from today were educated by the same liberal professors who so happened to be the flower power love-children, and latch-key kids of the former hippie generation. The same people who also either failed to learned the bill of rights, or deliberately conspired to remove them. These disoriented victims of child-abuse were dragged around America in the back of a VW Combie, while their parents went to go 'find themselves'. What is evidently clear, is that they all adopted communism to support their lazy habits, and justify a wasted life. It is my opinion that the drug LSD is still coursing through their veins, as no rationally-minded person would invest their lives in believing in pseudo-science, climate change, gender fluidity or the new idiotic, oxymoron 'democratic' socialism.

THE END IS NIGH

Be warned. The tech elites will win this culture war, mark my words. They're too powerful, too integrated into our lives to ever be broken apart. The youth is our future, and the majority of our children are all imbibing the false rhetoric, and dangerous lies served by the looney left. It's a scary thought to think that the overwhelming consensus of youth believe that de-platforming alternative speech is a virtue, and group-think is paramount. Free speech will not prevail in a tech-ridden landscape, but will only survive in private quarters, for a while. It is evident that privacy scares the elites, which is why Google, Amazon and now Apple have created devices to listen in on you and your family. It's an ingenious idea, and highly conniving. By creating a tech dependent society, the 'food-eaters' will adopt even more invasive devices to spy on them, all for the reason to break down privacy. By diluting it, it no longer has meaning. Big Tech knows that it's impossible to gauge the enemy without constant intel to put oneself at an advantage. This explains the incessant compulsion for Silicon Valley to reap as much information from your personal life as possible. Not surprisingly, privacy is anathema according to the communist manifesto. All your thoughts, secrets and desires belong to the state. Therefore, by default we are living in a communist society already.

With the growing restrictions on free speech in America, all that remains for Big Tech's total takeover of the last great country in the world is to remove the second amendment. Around the time Bush Snr was giving his saccharine speech on world order aspirations, the elites were already devising diabolical plans to disarm, pacify and silence the masses. While the second amendment will always remain a thorn in their flesh, the liberal elites have created the concept of social media monitoring to legally spy on citizens. Through the creation of 'emojis', A.I is able to detect who is a candidate for revolt, which makes it easier to impose the dreaded 'mental illness' tag on dissidents. Ever wondered why Facebook is awash with cute animal videos topping millions of views? The reason is that most will always click the 'happy face' emoji to feel connected to the hive-mind. The dissident however will refuse. Keep smiling, and you'll be safe. Stop smiling, and you're a liability. Simply put, by law, liabilities are not allowed to purchase arms 'for their own safety'.

In the USA, a seemingly innocuous bill is being proposed in government which will require citizens to pass prerequisites to purchase arms according to their social media accounts standing, and to hand over their passwords for the authorities to inspect for unapproved thoughts. I promise you, this is not a fabricated conspiracy theory. It is entirely real, and it's a scary, Orwellian, and wholly Marxist concept devised by the the left. What's more confronting, is that those who are pro-gun, pro-Trump and Christian undoubtedly will be denied their second amendment right. After all, think back to what I just said about 'mental illness'. Those who are deemed unstable, or believe in a 'fictitious God' must be mentally ill. The View's Joy Behar already let the cat out of the bag by heralding this mentality, especially after her attack on Vice President Mike Pence, whom she called 'mentally ill' for believing in God. If that bill passes, Pence, and every other red-blooded American Christian will be exempt from exercising their constitutional right to bear arms. It's such an insidious and disgusting plan, but it looks to take over the west.

Moreover when government and big Pharma are working side and by side. Under Trump's administration, the cost of meds, including antidepressants have plummeted. This has been a landmark accomplishment for the billionaire elitist former developer. But the plan is simple. Get everyone on psyche meds, classify them as mentally ill, and presto! Your right to bear arms is gone. We can understand now why the west is quickly focusing on the issue of 'depression' in society. It's natural that people are feeling down, considering the liberals' constant push to create a hell-on earth situation. Who wouldn't want to reach for the pills? But this is all a part of a 'big idea', as Bush Snr called it. Indeed, order will arise out of chaos. Ladies and gentlemen, this is the ultimate plan for the liberals goal called 'gun control'.

Ironically however, liberals who naturally hate guns and somehow trust the state explicitly through naivety and ignorance, will be certainly allowed to purchase arms. They who created the elitist communist system in the west, won't need the arms to fight back. It's their world, they are the masters. Thus is the idiotic, catch-22 mindset of the Marxist elite today. And it's working to their advantage. This might be straight out of Orwell's '1984', and a reality in communist countries, as no citizen has the right to purchase any firearm, as the government perceives them to be a threat to the establishment - however, today this is coming to America.

In light of these draconian, insidious laws, the most glaring questions remain. When they take the guns, what other constitutional rights will they remove? How long before we expect to see liberal, paramilitary soldiers billeting in our homes with the state's permission? Will we see the re-introduction of cruel and unusual punishment? I believe it's not a matter of if, but when. One can only imagine just how dark the future will be under the elites' vision of a 'new world order'. Moreover when Islam begins to takeover the west through overpopulation. It's a statistical fact that Muslims outnumber westerners in terms of birthrate at around 5-1. In twenty years, the west will certainly be a different place. Orientalized, Orwellian, outlandish.

It is inevitable that systemic jihad will once again become just another part of daily life. I envision the truthers of this world, who will become the persecuted, will undoubtedly be forced to beg for food after private banks close their accounts for not conforming, and being 'hateful'. I believe, with the incorporation of Sharia and Marxist principles, dissidents will be forced to pay the Jizya tax and accept a global mark under threat of starvation. This of course conforms to the U.N's Agenda 21 policy of regionalisation and the removal of private farmers from the land. By controlling the food and energy supply, all will have to bow down to this coming world order; a universal state, steeped in the legacy of Big Tech.

Financial tyranny might seem like it's a long way off, but it's already happening today with private firms like Chase Manhattan Bank, Paypal, Patreon and Mastercard purging conservatives from their businesses. Perhaps there will come a day in a world of a monitored internet, where the remnant of freedom will be forced to meet in secrecy to spread the truth. God have mercy on us if we're caught, flown to a secret, quasi-military base, tortured at a black site secret prison, where we will face eventual re-education, or decapitation. Again, this is not science-fiction as we are seeing the preliminary stages of virtual Gulags occurring in Germany, and the advent of a 'name and shame' culture, where pariahs are being displayed to the public as the antithesis of 'love' and progressivism.

But where is the church and the catechism in all of this? In truth, the Catholic Church has been a deplorable example of Christ's word. The current pope, a traitor to God's word, and a closet Marxist hailing from a communist ridden continent, apparently believes that Islam is peaceful, that destabilising countries through mass migration is a virtue, and that there is no hell. Well, without hell, we can understand why the elitist technocrats have become so emboldened. Without eternal consequence and punishment, evil will certainly prevail. The Bible talks about the end days where 'doctrines of devils' will increase. With such 'holy men' as the pope, we can see that prophecy already is being fulfilled.

THE DEATH OF LIBERTY

The constitution is in crisis. There is no doubt about that. The reality is that the west, albeit all countries being ostensibly sovereign, naturally adopt American cultural normalities, which are based on the bill of rights. If America falls, we all do. The American constitution is the natural extension of God's laws, and a right that millions have fought and died to protect. It is through American culture which positively affects western institutions into adopting a more libertarian approach to the free market, expression, and dignity. In reality, the bill of rights, the constitution, puts other western countries to shame in regards to true freedom.

The land of the free, the home of the brave. That used to be the case. Today, it's a whole different matter. As we can see, there is a steady decline in western liberties throughout the USA, predominantly centralised in the liberal nerve-centres like California, Oregon and Washington state. As the Hollywood media reaches hundreds of millions around the world, its left-leaning propaganda wielding machine is setting the dangerous trend for a dystopian, socialist nightmare about to appear on the horizon. As America goes deeper down the rabbit hole, we therefore see the same sick standards naturally transferred to other western countries. America was once the moral vanguard, the shining example to follow, as it preserved the rights of the common man. Britain was a close second. As I have already highlighted in the previous chapter, the land called Great Britain is no longer worthy of such a title. And in some way, as I already explained, the UK has been the forefront in creating an insidious cultural trend towards socialistic values, and the theatre of the absurd. It is America's close knit ties, or used to be, which explains why the liberal states throughout the USA are copying the same bizarre antics inspired by the British. In some way, both the UK and the west coast American states share a symbiotic relationship in destroying the fabric of western society. They feed off each other perfectly, and are doing so harmoniously while the world becomes a living hell around them.

While the UK is within reaching distance of permanently converting into a communist regime, America on the other hand is going to prove to be a challenge for Marxists. That being said, it's not entirely impossible, or unfeasible. If any American in the 1950s were to see their country today, they would be truly horrified, disappointed and scared out of their wits. I would say the initial shock would be the cultural changes that have occurred, the lack of probity, common decency and big government. But as cultures come and go, the United States has always been a sovereign nation built on the freedom given from the bill of rights. Therefore, I believe anyone from the golden age would be more disgusted with the violation of the constitution, then the sordid display of liberal values propagated today. Who would believe in this day and age that a wealth of the bill of rights are under attack, if not already nullified through cultural passivity and apathy? The founding fathers would be rolling in their graves if they saw the condition of their beautiful country, and the blessed piece of work they fought to protect.

Let us evaluate our remaining freedoms under the bill of rights.

Amendment 1
- Freedom of Religion, Speech, and the Press

Congress shall make no law respecting an establishment of religion or prohibiting the free exercise thereof, or abridging the freedom of speech or of the press, or the right of the people peaceably to assemble and to petition the government for a redress of grievances.

Perhaps the most important amendment, for obvious reasons, it guarantees us the right to criticize our leaders, elected and unelected, and to freely express ourselves legally, and religiously, without limitations. Of course, this is no longer the case. Our speech is becoming prohibited, and if not, it's abridged. Alternative and conservative press no longer see the same equality of access as the left-wing media does. We're also witnessing a lack of transparency in government, where the authorities thwart any complete investigation into corruption and interference. This is not how a free country works to aid a free press. This is tyranny, pure and simple.

As the amendment states, free assembly is a right. But not in America anymore. If any conservative is to publicly state their case, they're met with harassment, threats by the looney left, and eventual seizure by the police for apparently 'disturbing the peace', when it's the liberals who cause the disruption. Whenever a conservative journalist camps outside a liberal senator's house on public land, the police then escort or arrest said activist on trumped up charges. Lord help them if they're a Christian protesting Planned Parenthood, the systemic genocide of innocent babies. After all, killing babies in the USA is big business. This is not what the founding fathers had in mind. And it is a disgrace what is happening in the USA today.

Amendment 2
- The Right to Bear Arms

A well-regulated Militia being necessary to the security of a free State, the right of the people to keep and bear Arms shall not be infringed.

The Marxists in government have tried everything to nullify this amendment, and they're not going to stop. And why would they? It's the last line of defence for a free republic against a ravenous, cabal in DC, who don't have the guts to just come out and declare themselves as communists. The second amendment was created precisely for this reason. It is to protect against government tyranny, a corrupt police force, roving gangs in a lawless world, and against corporate-governmental dictatorships. The ghouls in DC know that their communist, subversive antics won't last for long with the average red-blooded American packing heat. We voted them in, but we can get them out, forcibly if necessary. The people are forgetting that they have the executive powers to remove people in office, not the government. The constitution was created for the people, of the people, and by the people. Not to serve the government alone. And this scares the power hungry elite on Capitol Hill. I call all patriots to be vigilant and prepared. The liberal agenda is on the move, and we haven't seen the worst to come… only just a taste.

For example, during the 2020 election race, candidate Kamala Harris declared her intention to criminalise private gun sales via 'executive action' if elected. This is a bold statement, and virtually renders the second amendment obsolete. The delusion runs thick with the liberal elites, but they just might be crazy enough to get away with it. By conning the public with false flag attacks, negative press, and the denigration of American heritage, it's only a matter of time before red-blooded Americans rethink their stance on the sacred second amendment. Propaganda is a powerful tool, and therefore we must renew our minds daily and think critically.

Amendment 3
- The Housing of Soldiers

No soldier shall, in time of peace, be quartered in any house without the consent of the owner, nor in time of war but in a manner to be prescribed by law.

While the globalists haven't yet violated this amendment, it's highly possible that this will occur in the near future. We've already seen the government test the waters with National Guard billeting, which is a violation that was addressed in Engblom v Carey. With constant rumours of war, the EU's desire to build a continental army with the intentions of invasion, and with an Iran conflict on the horizon, it's inevitable that billeting will take shape soon. While many will scoff at this notion, I remind that it wasn't so long ago that President Obama declared that he intended to create a paramilitary youth brigade which would patrol the United States in the name of security. This organisation was called the Obama Youth Corp, similar in style to the Hitler Youth.

In the near future, it wouldn't be unfeasible that this communist style of state security would necessitate the need for unofficial 'soldiers' to be housed across the country, as a national draft is enacted for 'national security'. Moreover, with military bases already full with real 'soldiers', paramilitary groups will have no choice but to billet on private land. With Russia playing the bogeyman for the last twenty years, and the elites' constant fear-mongering of WWIII, I doubt anyone could deny that the government would impose themselves on the people through such insidious ways.

Amendment 4
- Protection from Unreasonable Searches and Seizures

The right of the people to be secure in their persons, houses, papers, and effects against unreasonable searches and seizures shall not be violated, and no warrants shall issue but upon probable cause, supported by oath or affirmation, and particularly describing the place to be searched and the persons or things to be seized.

Ostensibly, the U.S government cannot search American houses, papers and effects without a warrant. However, the echelon has already violated this amendment by illegally spying on citizens' data, possessions and their homes through the NSA's secret surveillance program which was exposed by whistleblower Edward Snowden. While the program might have been censured, it is simply naive to believe that the US government would not continue to abuse Big Tech resources to spy on the individual, and ultimately negate the fourth amendment.

Big Tech was actually created by the CIA. And if you don't believe me, I suggest you do your own research. Google, perhaps the most pernicious spy agency on the planet, was funded directly by the taxpayer, straight from Langley, VA. The company itself acts as a backdoor to collating data without warrants to use against the masses. This is already occurring with Google's Home device, and similarly, Amazon's Alexa, where both have been caught out for listening to customers' conversations.

With Big Tech facilitating an age where privacy is no longer sacred, we can understand why the Trump administration has been tepid to investigate citizen spying. As Bush Snr put it, 'it's a big idea, a new world order.' You can't rule the world without violating the bill of rights. And eroding this particular amendment is paramount in establishing a communist world government.

Amendment 5
- Protection of Rights to Life, Liberty, and Property

No person shall be held to answer for a capital or otherwise infamous crime unless on a presentment or indictment of a grand jury, except in cases arising in the land or naval forces, or in the militia, when in actual service in time of war or public danger; nor shall any person be subject for the same offense to be twice put in jeopardy of life or limb; nor shall be compelled in any criminal case to be a witness against himself, nor be deprived of life, liberty, or property without due process of law; nor shall private property be taken for public use without just compensation.

The flagrant disregard for this amendment is disgusting. The United States has already gone down a dark path by breaking a number of statutes within this bill. For starters, citizens are now being deprived of natural liberty such as free speech and religion. This we already know. However, with the Trump administration's goal to introduce a national I.D, mandatory for domestic travel, this alone will violate the amendment and one's right to liberty and mobility. The constitution never states that we must carry identification at all times, especially to travel regionally. That's communism defined. What will we see in the USA next? Paramilitary officials screaming 'papers please!'?

The amendment's support for due process is one of the most important rights a US citizen can have. But ever since 9/11, the dreaded Patriot Act has been wielded as a broadsword to sweep people off the streets and fly them to CIA black sites indefinitely for torture. Citizens caught in this situation have no access to a lawyer, and none are provided by the state. The deprivation of their liberties is all for big business, and to create the illusion that America is constantly under attack. Torturing any citizen on off-shore facilities is egregious. Again, this is gulag style, communist punishment. And just to think, the American taxpayer is funding this.

Amendment 6
- Rights of Accused Persons in Criminal Cases

In all criminal prosecutions, the accused shall enjoy the right to a speedy and public trial by an impartial jury of the state and district wherein the crime shall have been committed, which district shall have been previously ascertained by law, and to be informed of the nature and cause of the accusation; to be confronted with the witnesses against him; to have compulsory process for obtaining witnesses in his favor; and to have the assistance of counsel for his defense.

The court system today is a joke. Overly bloated and bureaucratic, designed to bleed the plaintiff and defendant equally of finances and precious time. Speedy trials are now an antiquated form of jurisprudence, as lengthy court battles are to benefit the system, lawyers and their cronies. Have you ever met a poor lawyer? I haven't. They're all living off people's misery, and grinning all the way to the bank. Speedy trials do not give ambulance chasing scum the opportunity to profit of lawsuits, which is why the sixth amendment has deliberately been molested to accomodate unethical and immoral ghouls.

A civil lawsuit today, where the plaintiff is suing the government for violating their rights, can take years in the court system. God help them if they run out of money. Their cause could be finished before it's started. The government knows this, and will do everything to hinder an application through unconstitutionally excessive fees, bureaucratic interference, and legal intimidation. Today, the term 'chequebook justice', implies whoever has the most money wins. And it most certainly is the case, which explains why so many poor people suffer, and the rich just get away with murder. That is not natural justice, and is an affront to this amendment. Certainly, it is not what the founding fathers envisioned, especially how the government wields 'lawsuits' as a weapon to punish innocent individuals. You see, the government can afford to throw a barrage of lawyers your way. After all, it's your tax that's paying for them anyway. Even if you win, you've had to pay from your earnings for the loss of time and stress. And if you lose, they'll bankrupt you by forcing you to pay their legal fees. I remind the reader what happened to General Michael Flynn during Mueller's and the deep state's Russian hoax witch trial. The man lost everything over a supposed lie. This is how the government are punishing people these days, and it flies in the face of the sixth amendment.

Finally, the amendment expresses that public trials must be by an impartial jury. But as recent history shows, state prosecution teams are notorious for swinging the decision in their favour by rigging juries based on politics, race, and preconceived biases. The same can be said about defence lawyers who protect criminals, likewise by working with a prejudiced jury to seek acquittal. We've seen this already occur numerous times, especially with high profile trials such as California v O.J Simpson. As we now know, the trial was a sham, with the state begrudgingly accepting a near all black jury towards the end of the spectacle, for the sake of political correctness. And we all know how that turned out. Two murdered souls went unavenged. This alone was a violation of the sixth. But, the public was more concerned with race than their own rights being flushed down the toilet.

Nothing is perfect in an imperfect world. I understand this. But the lack of probity in the USA today is staggering. At least the judiciary could at least try to appeal to the sixth amendment. But like all corrupt industries, they've sold out. God help us all.

Amendment 7
- Rights in Civil Cases

In suits at common law, where the value in controversy shall exceed twenty dollars, the right of trial by jury shall be preserved, and no fact tried by a jury shall be otherwise reexamined in any court of the United States than according to the rules of the common law.

The bloated legal system today is designed to bankrupt aggrieved plaintiffs and victimised defendants alike. It's a weaponised system of bureaucracy that breaks the common man, and rewards the corrupt. As the amendment states, 'no fact tried by a jury shall be reexamined'. Today, this is simply not the case. Indeed, cases are being retried under appeal, again and again, in an array of courts until the victim never gets justice. We have district courts, the magistrates court, court of appeals, tribunals. The whole thing is a joke. Even if the plaintiff appeals and fights fire with fire, the judiciary will continually throw doubt on the evidence, and feed it through the judicial meat grinder, where the weight of justice becomes so insignificant, that rulings become less than perfunctory. And then we have corrupt judges. If you're lucky enough to win by the skin of your teeth, another judge in another court will hear the case again, and then throw it out.

Of course, this doesn't apply to the mega rich who can afford to abuse the system to line their pockets, or avoid jail time altogether with a slap on the wrist. It's called 'turnstile justice'. And it's been happening ever since the rich got richer, and the poor got poorer. Yes, the seventh amendment is now invalid. The corrupt government and its judiciary are moving the goal posts farther away when the plaintiff looks to win. Make no mistake, just because you're debt free, they will come for your property through the corrupt legal system. Be warned.

Amendment 8
- Excessive Bail, Fines, and Punishments Forbidden

Excessive bail shall not be required, nor excessive fines imposed, nor cruel and unusual punishments inflicted.

Anyone who has a modicum of knowledge over public trials can already see that the eighth amendment is now invalid. As it states, no citizen shall have excessive bail costs or fines imposed on them. Over the last twenty years, we have seen corrupt judges wielding their gavel like a weapon, and setting astronomical bail costs on the subject. Historically speaking, bail has been set in the millions of dollars in some cases, which is not uncommon. Likewise, excessive fines seem to be common place in the courts, especially over civil infractions which would not exist over fifty years ago. The more the USA becomes a bureaucratic mess, the more citizens are in risk of violating invisible laws that will draw immense fines. This is simply unconstitutional and is an affront to what the founding fathers stood for. Do you really believe that Washington himself envisioned that America would become a bureaucratic, bloated, rapacious, punitive system of control over the masses? No. The country that the first settlers fled, represented the exact system of constriction that we are living under today.

On the issue of cruel and unusual punishment, the USA might not officially engage in such acts on American soil, but we all know how the Patriot Act allows the government to unconstitutionally detain and fly out suspects to black sites. It is there that these facilities are set up to launder people, and to torture them to death or to confession. It goes to show that our court system and judiciary is now a runaway, corrupt institution who are playing by their own rules.

Amendment 9
- Other Rights Kept by the People

The enumeration in the Constitution of certain rights shall not be construed to deny or disparage others retained by the people.

While the terminology and meaning behind this amendment does seem a little confusing, it's quite simple. Basically speaking, the rights of man in a free republic, does not end with the constitution. The ninth's amendment shows a belief in the constitution's authors that fundamental rights exist that are not expressly listed in the first eight amendments. In simple terms, the ninth prevents the average American's liberties from being constricted within the constitution. Freedom is freedom. You can't limit it, no matter how exhaustive the context. The ninth was to prevent tyrannical governments confining citizens to these first eight alone.

However, our government and judiciary today are already violating this amendment, by seeking to evermore restrict people's liberties through unbridled bureaucracy, and unnecessary laws to clamp down on American freedom. The corrupt courts' deliberate obtusity to reason with the plaintiff over the expansion of more freedoms is compelling. Instead, we are seeing a retroactive move to shrink liberties back down to the original, and even then, hinder them entirely. This being, speech, worship, mobility, prosperity, privacy, and access to the law. This is the globalist's insidious plan, and it's happening right now.

Amendment 10
- Undelegated Powers Kept by the States and the People

The powers not delegated to the United States by the Constitution, nor prohibited by it to the states, are reserved to the states respectively, or to the people.

The tenth amendment supports federalism, but upholds state autonomy as priority to prevent against government overreach and dictatorships. Most importantly, it emphasises the crucial foundation that the state is controlled by the people. What we can see is that the globalist elite are molesting this amendment in a number of ways. Their agenda is somewhat of a contradiction of their own politics, but necessary for their agenda to seek fruition. Firstly, they are abusing the tenth by virtually breaking away from federal control through their constant resistance against a conservative government. While the amendment supports state autonomy to certain degrees, it is for the discretion over laws, not culture. What we can see is unjustified cultural militancy over cultural normativity, which is misconstrued as a tenth amendment privilege, when it is not.

However, once the globalists abuse this amendment to seize power, only then will they attempt to negate the tenth after creating a federal, immutable government dictatorship, where state autonomy will be outlawed. I believe they will accomplish this using the 'love' card. We can see the cultural shift today where those who defy globalist rule are deemed 'unloving'. We've all heard the term 'we're stronger together', and it applies here. Most certainly, universal federalism is the beginning for globalists. The end goal is a totalitarian communist state which eventually overthrows federalism, and the tenth amendment. If you were to doubt this ever happening, or government overreach to violate the tenth, think back to the Obama administration's enactment of Obamacare; a federal Marxist healthcare program. Despite being wholly unconstitutional in every way, it was forced through the federal health system, regardless. That's only the beginning. I predict that new 'federal' laws will be introduced soon to take away your right to bear arms, under the pretence of 'love', false peace and universal security.

The power of the state no longer belongs to the people. You're being told what to do, instead of the other way around. The government no longer seems to be serving the people, or interested in doing so. We are being reigned over. What is evident, is that America is now a rich man's game, and the government is investing itself in corporate businesses with communist principles. The bill of rights only protect those with political power, celebrity influence, and who are of the blue blood line.

All I can say is this...

Know your rights, defend them at all costs (non-violently of course), while you can. The people you continue to vote for have no

191

interest in your well-being, your dignity and your children's future. The whole election process is a sham, and is a stage for the next puppet President to be called out on cue to pull apart the fabric of our society.

The only thing that stands between the globalists and total world domination, is the US constitution. They who want to kill us are working hard to break it down, piece by piece, until the entire document is nullified. For when freedom falls, the ghouls will take control by default, and reign over us with impunity. This is not fiction, but wholly historical, as we saw the rise of Hitler through identical means. We must remember that Hitler seized power by creating a false flag attack to allow him to enact 'emergency powers' at the expense of civil liberties and to abolish the constitution. This is not different to how Obama signed the NDAA for 'national security', which permits the military to sweep people off the streets, much the same way as how the gestapo and SS controlled the populous.

Just as we are seeing our countries implode, the fall of pre-Nazi Germany came suddenly, and calculatingly. The following excerpt demonstrates how the German constitution became nullified in only a few hours, all through 'national security'.

> On the night of Feb. 27, 1933 the Reichstag
> building was set on fire. At the urging of Hitler,
> Hindenburg responded the next day by issuing an
> emergency decree "for the Protection of the people
> and the State," which stated: "Restrictions on
> personal liberty, on the right of free expression of
> opinion, including freedom of the press; on the
> rights of assembly and association; and violations of
> the privacy of postal, telegraphic and telephonic

communications and warrants for house searches, orders for confiscations as well as restrictions on property, are also permissible beyond the legal limits otherwise prescribed."

- Encyclopedia Britannica

This is your final warning.

THE VOICE OF REASON

After reading through the bill of rights, and how they've been nullified steadily over the years, it's hard to believe that we've come to this. How far will the elites go? What else will they do? When all the guns have been banned, and when all the words have been censored, when history has been erased, and all the freedoms you took for granted have been taken, only then will we fully appreciate what we once had. Only by then, it will be too late.

I close this chapter with the words of Tucker Carlson, who delivered a very powerful speech in 2019 over the loss of freedoms in America, surprisingly under President Trump. Here is what he had to say.

"People voted for Donald Trump believing that they would have more of it (freedom of speech). Two years in, the opposite has happened. A ruling class has clamped down as never before on personal expression. Gone is the free exchange of ideas we were promised as Americans, it was supposed to be our birthright. In its place now, mandatory, soul-deadening, conformity. An entire

population forced to repeat the same mindless platitudes, or else. An axis of left-wing corporate power, academia, the media, and lawmakers, have all aligned to curb your right to speak freely, which is to say, the right to think for yourself. When they control your words, they control your mind. The left used to deny that it was their goal, they're not pretending anymore. They're bearing their teeth and snarling. Get in line, or we'll hurt you. Apple CEO pledged that Apple, one of the most powerful companies in the history of the world, will do whatever it takes to silence dissenting opinion. Hate is the word they used for views they don't like, or questions they can't answer. The liberal message is simple. We are holy, you are fallen. Shut up and obey. CEOs didn't use to talk like this. They were in the business of selling products, not preaching sermons. Then over time, conventional religion ceded from public life. Liberals then stepped forward to fill that void. It was not an upgrade. Apple, Google and Big Tech combined have more power than the church ever had, despite having much less humility, and restraint. Leaders a hundred years ago could tolerate dissent. There was a reverence to God to fix societies problems through his wisdom. The modern ruling class however, consider themselves as God. They render their own judgment, where disagreement is equivalent to apostasy. Like Islam, uncooperation is an attack on the one true faith."
- Tucker Carlson, Fox News

If you agree with this statement, as I most surely do, read the next chapter on how you can begin to take back your country, and do so without violence.

PLAN OF ACTION

It's no secret that Big Tech is way out of control. And if their narcissistic ethos of intolerant totalitarianism continues unchecked, it won't take a genius to see how bad this world will become. We have witnessed the ultimate power they wield to control nation states, and how easy it is for them to destroy and erase individuals who fail to conform. No other empire, civilisation or king in history has ever brandished the same power the cronies in Silicon Valley possess today. What is certainly more unnerving, is that almost every tech company coming out of San Jose, most importantly the gang of four, are indeed colluding together. Not in secret, but in full view of the entire world. Group-think, gang-related, techno thuggery is their modus operandi, and all beneath them are being forced to change their ways to fit in with the new world standard.

As we can see, we are slowly losing our grip on the world. We the people are no longer the masters of our own destiny, but are being herded together like cattle, and fed the Marxist doctrine of servitude under tyranny. I personally have no desire to go down without a fight, and I will not live in a world dictated by unelected, communist thugs, posing as latte-sipping hipsters. Therefore, I have included in this chapter a complete list of objectives for you, the rebel, to take note of. This will give you an edge over our soon to be overlords, and with God's help, may very well win the culture war we are already experiencing. Let us begin.

FIGHT BIG TECH WITH CLASSIFICATION LAWS

Many, including our politicians, have strongly implied that Big Tech is in breach of antitrust laws. For the layman, these laws were implemented for the very reason of preventing monopolies in certain markets and industries, for fair competition and to stop tyrannical companies which look to subvert the government, which is the people. The antitrust argument is problematic, in that all of Big Tech is not completely in violation of the law in that regard. They are private entities, albeit colluding with each other, but every tech company shares equal market share with their 'competitors', lest for one, Google.

In terms of web search and video upload services, Google wins hands down. And by far, out of the big four, it is certainly guilty of antitrust. It has become too big, too fast, and looks to take over the world in terms of cultural manipulation, and election rigging. In the EU, Google has already received enormous fines over its antitrust violations, but the company doesn't look like it's going anywhere soon. In 2019, the US department of justice has already filed an application to investigate the company over antitrust. It is my personal belief that breaking up this company will do no good in the long run, and for reasons I will explain in a moment.

Nonetheless, the other two major contributors to the problem, Facebook and Twitter, somewhat evade antitrust laws as each maintain an equal and healthy competition with each other. None maintain full market dominance in terms of social media platforms. If the market is split by 50-50, it's hard to hold them accountable. Think upon Microsoft and Apple, Sony and Samsung. It's the same thing. The problem with Facebook is that, like Google, it too is encouraging existing users to sign in to third party accounts and websites with the platform. However, if your Facebook account is suspended for 'hate speech', or trumped up charges, you will lose all access to these websites. Some of which might maintain financial records or crucial data. Therein lies the problem.

So, to summarize, Google and Youtube together are indeed in breach of antitrust. Facebook and Twitter, not so much. Nonetheless, there is hope in bringing these companies down and retaining our right to free speech. To fight Big Tech, we must push our government to not solely focus on antitrust technicalities and loopholes, but approach the problem with a simple method. Publishing vs utility. As a free and sovereign nation, where all are protected under discrimination laws, we must implore our government to force Big Tech companies to classify themselves as utility services, not as publishers.

Publishers, by definition, have control over the content on their platform, to comply with decency laws. This is the ostensible reason why Big Tech is scrambling to erase material which is purported to be 'offensive', but in reality, is ill-fitting with liberal standards; in other words, liabilities to their cause. You see, a private publishing company technically has the legal right to control what people see on its platform, regardless if they do so with brutal discrimination. It's their company, they can do whatever they want. However, the problem that lies with Big Tech, is that through global infiltration and mass communication, they are no longer classified as a publisher, but a utility. Utilities such as ISPs, telcos, energy monoliths, or perhaps even your local taxi company, have no right to dictate what information, content, or even person is allowed to use, or transfer material over their services (with the exception of illicit content). To deny access to any service, no matter privately owned, would constitute as discrimination.

Therefore, these laws would irrevocably apply to the gang of four, and there is nothing they could do about it.

They can protest and run with the 'publisher' defence all day, but the fact is that literally billions of people are using their services to communicate, build relationships, date, share ideas, collaborate on work projects and to organise political interests. These companies have no right to listen to your conversations, or to manipulate end-users from distancing themselves from other people. Their utility network is now public access, just like your telephone, regardless if it's privatized. Imagine for a second if your phone provider closed your account for condemning abortions. Or try to envision your energy company switching off your power for running a conservative party's internet server. Simply put, under US law, they have no right to do so. Again, this is why Big Tech are vehemently against classifying themselves as a utility, and profusely put out the cover story, the lie that they are a publisher. Of course, if they lose their publisher status, they lose the primary ability to brainwash the masses, which is the whole reason they set up their platform in the first place.

Sadly, because of Big Tech's pompous arrogance in believing they have the moral right to ruin lives, financial institutions have followed suit through the herd mentality. While these private banking and finance companies do not provide content to the public, and customers' financial affairs are kept private, they have jumped on the bandwagon to close down people's credit cards, banking accounts and more, all for being a conservative. As I have previously mentioned, financial services such as Paypal, Patreon, Mastercard, GoDaddy, Chase Manhattan Bank and more are all guilty of this crime. They need to be stopped, lest we see more people's lives ruined on a liberal whim. But alas, as this trend of tech tyranny grows in the financial sector, it gives us an insight into how desperate they have become through detrimentally affecting their business by shunning prospective customers. You see, this is no longer about money, but control. Big Tech and the financial industries have accrued so much wealth, that it's inconsequential to them to reap another billion or so. It is evident that their quarterly stock market meetings are based on political purges, and cleaning up society of 'racism', 'bigotry', 'homophobia' and 'xenophobia'. It's staggering to see that stock holders are willing to forgo stock increases by investing in companies that have more interest in politics, than the almighty dollar. If this wasn't true, investors would be pulling their money out of such risky ventures, quicker than you can say 'pinko!'

So, how can we prevent tech and financial tyranny from spreading like the cancer it is? Well, quite simply, the government must get tougher on institutions that are heavily invested in dismantling the constitution and people's liberties. While Big Tech might feign disinterest in financial gains, the bottom line is that these monoliths cannot function without money. Take away their piggy banks, and they're nothing. Besides, what hardline, firebrand liberal employee would be so dedicated to further the Marxist cause without an annual salary? They might be communist at heart, but rent isn't cheap. Therefore, I believe the quickest solution is to impose massive fines on companies, and their owners. In the past, the government has successfully sued companies for environmental disasters, which have seen the industry cleaned up. Why can't the same methodology be applied to Big Tech? By imposing immense fines on tech companies, the government, who is acting on behalf of the people, is directly reducing the salary and net worth of the gang of four CEOs. For the layman, we must understand that Zuckerberg, Dorsey and Pichai have all reached an astronomical status of wealth through reinvestment of their salaries into tech stocks. As their companies continue to profit, so do they. In a way, it's sort of a Ponzi scheme, but I won't elaborate on that just yet.

Finally, the government must close the tax loophole which has allowed Big Tech to escape taxation for years. According to records, Google and Facebook pay little to no tax, which is somewhere around a few million dollars on top of billions in profits. Cayman Island off-shore banks hold the majority of Big Tech's wealth, and these quasi-legal tax laws need to be eradicated. If they are American based, they should pay American tax. This is another mystery why Trump has not bothered to prevent this from happening, considering his financially prudent mandate. I guarantee, once Big Tech starts to see their net worth become reduced by as much as 30% in only a few years, they will abandon their Marxist ties, and focus on profit through public accessibility, like they used to.

You never reward a child's bad behaviour.

SUPPORT STRICTER CITIZENSHIP LAWS

America, and the west, is indeed a land for the free. We embrace people of all faiths and cultures, but somehow have forgotten it is our culture which should take prominence. Not through oppression, but through pride. Sadly, communist propaganda and liberal brainwashing have resulted in our youth shunning this precedent, where they now childishly resort to histrionically labelling patriots as racists. Well, they can call us whatever they want, but the fact is that this is still our land, our civilisation, our society. If immigrants desire to live under oppressive, corrupt, kangaroo court ruled countries, so be it. Perhaps they would like to move to Saudi Arabia, North Korea, or communist China. In those countries, citizens need not worry themselves over free speech and thought. It's automatically done for them.

In our land, we have a constitution, the rule of law, a culture based on probity, and the inherent resistance to tyranny. We bear arms to protect against corruption and despotism, and we are promised the pursuit of happiness, not the guarantee. We are a nation that includes people of all walks of life, with different opinions, races and creeds. But we are all one, in that we believe in the right to live independently from forced political persuasion, and government dictatorships. Unfortunately, we are receiving a deluge of immigrants that don't see it our way, nor do they wish to contribute to the fabric of western society, but seek to colonise our nation with their own undemocratic culture. It is not racist to call this out as a cultural takeover, for what it truly is. **For those who have migrated here legally, invested their lives to raise their children to embrace the west, I welcome you with open arms.**

But for the people who migrate to our western countries, refuse to embrace the rule of law and the culture, are nothing but settlers. Not surprisingly, I am talking about those who have moved to the USA on work visas to be inducted into Silicon Valley. They have been hired from overseas, specifically for their radical views, and hailing from historically anti-western countries, which ultimately show no appreciation of democracy, the constitution, or the three hundred plus years of blood and sacrifice to establish and defend this great land. Sadly, it is at this nerve-centre that new migrants share a relationship with existing settlers who likewise fester in their hatred for the west, and further bring with them a whole string of ideas to subvert our government. It is only in the past ten years which has seen Big Tech transform into which was once a fun-loving, free and open industry, to a cold-hearted, mean-spirited, heavily orientalized, culturally Marxist, anti-west, think-tank. Moreover, immigrants who have moved on from Big Tech to work in the government sector, are also bringing their Marxist-aligned ways into the workplace, and corrupting the whole system through indolence and sabotage. This is not fiction, but wholly real. The media outlet 'Project Veritas' exposed the government infiltration of new migrants who admitted on hidden camera that they were working to undermine the government through subversion. It is my personal opinion that many who seek citizenship in the USA do not have the country's best interests in mind. I wouldn't go as far as to say 'sleeper cell', but it's certainly a term that comes to mind. Call this what you will, but this is treason.

This must stop.

Therefore, I believe we must get tougher on such criminals by automatically revoking their citizenship according to violations under a new probationary citizenship period of ten years. It's ridiculous that our governments dole out unconditional citizenships to unwilling participants to western standards, then stand idly when such people immediately shun their oath, and work to subvert our infrastructure. This flies in the face of the citizenship oath they swore to uphold, of which I highlighted earlier in this book. Like Sundar Pichai, CEO of Google, there are literally hundreds and thousands of new migrants who have already breached their oath by either working to destroy America, or even planning domestic jihad attacks. For acts such as terrorism, I believe that immediate revocation of citizenship is called for. Such people never intended to live peaceably in the USA, and need to be removed. In all fairness, certain western countries have already began procedures for automatic cancellation of citizenship for ISIS fighters, which is great news. But in reality, what is the difference between an ISIS fighter, and a CEO at Big Tech who seeks to subvert the constitution and meddle in national elections? For me, the latter also qualifies as terrorism. At least with the ISIS fighter, you know where you stand. With the passive-aggressive left, who perennially gaslight their victims, I would say liberalism is far more dangerous. In reality, both are traitors to their country, but somehow the hipster in Silicon Valley gets a pass, because it's trendy to persecute conservatives based on their religion. This is a travesty.

The problem that lies ahead is hardwiring into the public's mind the inescapable commonalities that liberalism shares with communism. Most people are completely unaware that liberalism and Marxism go hand in hand. And at the base level, practicing liberal progressivism is acceptable, but escalating that ideology through Marxist principles, which inevitably impinges on another citizen's rights, is where the government must draw the line. All migrants swore an oath to protect and defend the constitution, which entails preserving the liberty of the entire nation, not just a select elite. Liberals can protest all they like, but the USA is not a communist country, and it never will be. Liberals can rebrand the murderous, intolerant ideology as 'democratic socialism', but they're not fooling anyone. There is no room in any western country for subversive communists, who conceal their agenda under the guise of progressive liberalism. You can't expect Marxists to swear an oath to protect the constitution, when it is democratic, capitalistic principles which they aim to destroy.

KNOW YOUR RIGHTS AND THE LAW

With a growing police state, an out of control judiciary playing by their own rules, and a government who obviously doesn't care about the people, I can't stress enough that all should protect themselves legally. Knowing your civil rights and laws according to your state and local municipality is an imperative that must not be ignored. The law, although becoming less effective each day, is all we have left. It's what separates us from the animals, and prevents a thuggish police department from throwing their weight around to intimidate the public. Coercion through force seems to be the police's modus operandi today to usher in the new world government. And the people are simply following suit and standing in line to be lambs to the slaughter. In the words of Julian Assange, who indignantly screamed while being lifted off his feet to prison, "Resist! Resist! While you still can!" Stand your ground, know your rights, and remind them that they are to serve and protect, not dominate and harass.

The sheer amount of horror stories of police brutality and corruption that I have encountered in my years working as a journalist, is staggering. The one common trait among all victims is that they never stood their ground. They were too polite, and let the thugs run all over them. The police might be civil servants, sworn to protect, but in all honesty, I trust them as far as I can throw them. It is because of the public's ignorance of their rights, the confusion over civil and criminal distinctions, and the unknown limits of police jurisdiction and their powers, which have seen the people systematically being abused by corrupt officials. Don't become that person! Your rights and civil law is all accessible online, and in law libraries. If you are truly serious about protecting yourself from government overreach, then you will learn the basics about police protocol, their limits of jurisdiction, their powers, and legal terminology which will render the corrupt judiciary completely powerless. It's not impossible, as I have seen the law work effectively to put the out of control police in their place, and eventually fired.

I recall a particular case where the American judiciary and police had conspired to persecute a man over fishing rights, where the man was summoned to court on charges for allegedly breaking the law for simply fishing in the wild. The judge sat herself down, with a smug look on her face, and all had obviously underestimated the man's knowledge of state laws and human rights. What occurred was an embarrassing fiasco for the judge and her goons, as she was exposed for being a legal bully who boldly try to incarcerate the man on trumped up charges. The judge proceeded to read out the charges in the packed courtroom, when suddenly, the fifty-two year old man told the judge the simple facts, "I am a living man protected by natural law and I have the right to forage for food when I am hungry… You are trying to create a fictitious, fraudulent action."

The reaction was priceless. The judge, obviously not used to being given a dressing down, foolishly made matters worse. From the records, the judge came off looking like a nincompoop by threatening the accused with contempt of court. However, what the judge didn't realize was that the man was representing himself, so naturally anything he said was testimony, not "contempt" as such. In layman's terms, she was powerless to stop him. For obvious reasons, the man's temper increased, but he held strong and defied the ridiculous charges. As the judge fumbled about, completely gob-smacked, the middle-aged patriot simply stood up with his family, and just walked out the front door to their car, never to be seen again. Most probably, he went straight back to fishing. I wouldn't blame him. It was a beautiful thing to see the dictatorial government utterly powerless to reprimand or incarcerate the man, simply because he knew his rights and the law. If you were to see him in court, you would never have guessed he was legally savvy. But had he not stood his ground, used the law to its effect, he would be either serving time, or paying a hefty fine to a corrupt government - all for catching a fish to eat. This case was a classic example of government overreach and persecution over basic rights. And it is from that particular incident which inspired myself to become more vigilant legally.

You see, most people are overly trusting of the police today. It's instinctual, which has been passed down from our parents. Of course, back in the day, the constabulary was the citizen's best friend. Not so today. As social media spreads, we are becoming more aware of police overreach and blatant harassment. This has been exemplified with free speech activist and journalist, Tommy Robinson, whom has been targeted ruthlessly by the police for years. From witnessing Robinson's crusade, we can see that the UK government is unconstitutionally placing limitations on mobility, which is an egregious violation of human rights. However, in the USA, those freedoms are still enjoyed without impediment. For how long, nobody can be sure. While the UK is certainly a police state, with police falsely arresting citizens based on little probable cause or suspicion, all western citizens have the right to question if they're being arrested or detained. The common tactic for the police is to talk over you, recite irrelevant laws, in hopes that you will back down. This usually occurs during conservative rallies, or where liberals are losing the argument. Legally speaking, if the police do not let you be, you are being officially detained, but then the issue arises if they have suspicion to do so. In most cases, it's very little, and the police are simply flexing the muscles to intimidate. However, as a free citizen, you have the right to question while under temporary detention if you're being arrested. If the officer says 'no', then just walk away. Without suspicion or probable cause, they have no legal grounds to force you to answer any question if you don't want to, and cannot detain you further if they have no intention to arrest. At the moment they say 'no' to your inquiry, don't even ask 'can I go?' This empowers the police to further ask questions. Just walk away calmly and politely. This is basic law that people are unaware of. And it is one that infuriates the police to no end.

Of course, there are people who stand their ground by being rude to the police. While the first amendment does actually permit, it's not advisable. Firstly, you're better than that. It's bad enough a bent cop is harassing you for no reason, but you don't have to stoop to that level. Likewise, the police have no right to be discourteous and aggressive. While this is quite common in the service, if the police are being rude to you, just make a complaint to your local police station and record the incident. Chances are they'll be reprimanded, or even demoted if there are a number of complaints. If people don't complain, nothing will get done, and the corruption will continue.

It's evident that the police are becoming more prone to wielding their weight around to intimidate, banking on the ignorance of people. There is a wealth of videos online which demonstrate people fighting back peacefully, and standing up to police harassment. Of course, the other issue comes with the police recording your face. From my legal counsel's advice, I have been told that it's unconstitutional in America for the police to record your face without your permission. The fourth amendment makes it clear that the government will respect citizens' privacy, which includes the prohibition of unwanted, and excessive monitoring, especially without prior consent. I cannot comment for other western countries, but I would say that their constitution would protect citizens' privacy likewise. You would need to seek legal advice.

This is an important subject as in the last ten years, we have seen police increasingly wearing cameras on their person to record the public. As far as I know, the police have no right to film and record anyone, unless they are under arrest. Therefore, I would advise anyone who is unfortunate to be harassed by police to exercise their rights to privacy. If the police do not comply, simply cover your face. My legal counsel has advised that the police would be powerless to stop you from doing so. After all it's not illegal to wear a motorcycle helmet in public, and no officer can force you to remove it without warrant or arrest. Again, arrest must follow protocol with probable cause, suspicion and evidence. Naturally, to counter your resistance, the issue would then arise for the police to ask you for identification. US law states that no citizen need bear i.d in public, unless driving a car. If the police ask, you have the option of either giving your name, or refusing to comply based on the fourth amendment. Again, the police need probable cause or suspicion to arrest. It is your legal right to ask why you're being arrested, where you can then contest their assertion. If they refuse to reason, make sure to note if they read you the miranda warning; the list of your rights under federal law. If the police fail to inform you of your rights, which is highly uncommon, the case against you will be dismissed. Most people already know this, but be mindful.

Likewise, it's also most common for people who refuse to offer their identification to be handcuffed. But again, the police must offer their reason for detention or arrest. Obviously, the easiest way is to cooperate, but there is no telling how far the police will go if you do. Most probably they will want to check your person and effects, which is illegal without a warrant. Even if you do comply, you might be just arrested anyway for the sake of intimidation or harassment. If you're prepared to fight it out in court, the chances of you winning under 'wrongful arrest' and 'police harassment' are very good. After all, no officer wants to explain themselves before a judge why they randomly stopped an individual, arrested them on little evidence, forcefully slapped the cuffs on them, then hauled them downtown to be booked, fingerprinted and photographed, like a common criminal. The police department these days are running low on funds to pay out to innocent people. Again, if you know your rights, the police are powerless.

Indeed, the issue of citizen monitoring is becoming an irrevocable taboo that the public seem to be willing to go along with. A shocking revelation is that these 'security measures' are now being forced upon our children. In the UK, children in grade school are being digitally fingerprinted at the library for reading certain books. Had the draconian measures that we are witnessing today been implemented in the turn of the last century, the people would have revolted. It's just simply unconstitutional to record people incessantly in the name of 'security'. It is that kind of mentality which is executed in prisons, where rigorous monitoring with a manned security presence takes place. Likewise inmates are not free to walk from one end of the establishment to the other without permission. How does this differ from the society we're living in today? In a world where our western governments are quickly adopting the China-standard of security, which is facial tracking, limits of mobility and finance, I can easily say they do not have your best interests in mind.

The average person on the street is entirely law abiding. Almost nobody leaves their abode to commit a crime. The common individual is simply on their way to work, or to meet friends and family. Why the need for excessive government surveillance? Well, it's quite simple. With the steady increase of draconian laws, and new world government bureaucracy to be imposed on the people, it's inevitable that riots, revolts and attacks on state buildings will occur. Hence the need for more 'security'. The elites are making preparations to subdue, pacify, disarm the nation, and to allow them to play prison warden in the largest detention zone in this galaxy. They're doing this through the feminisation of men, gender role reversal, hate speech laws, and technological overreach. Most importantly, they're going to do it through the national i.d chip. This implant, which will derive from the smart phone, is inevitable to become an essential part of any human on this planet. Why do you think Big Tech is focusing more than ever on selling smart phones with facial scanning, and geographical tracking?

Of course, the public are just going along with the plan for the sake of convenience, but when will it end? In the last few years, we've become aware of 'voter fraud', which has been perpetrated by the Democrat party. Undocumented illegal immigrants are being encouraged to vote in state and presidential elections, which is giving the current government the impetus to implement a national i.d scheme for all US citizens. This is the first step in controlling the world. The Trump administration is also introducing the 'Real I.D' system by 2020 with facial scanning, under bill H.R.1268, for "Emergency supplemental appropriations act for defence, the global war on terror, or improved security for personal identification cards." This i.d system will incorporate the driver's license, permit, or identification card, and will be required to board commercial airplanes to travel domestically. As previously mentioned, it is unconstitutional for any government agency to ask a citizen to provide i.d for domestic air travel. You can get on a Greyhound bus without i.d, but not an airplane? Your person and luggage is scanned at the airport anyways, so why the need for further documentation? The bill of rights never states that a US citizen need carry i.d at all times, and we are protected by the fourth amendment. But somehow, the government seems to be conveniently forgetting this and are going full-steam ahead with their globalist plan.

My friends, do not comply through implied obligatory servitude. The government is meant to serve you, not the other way around. While you still can, I advise that you align yourself with a legal team that bases its practice solely on the constitution. Stand your ground. Form class action lawsuits against private firms for discrimination. By sticking together, we create strength in numbers, and will turn the tables against them.

Know your rights. Don't become sheep to the slaughter.

SPEAK THE TRUTH AND BE INDEPENDENT

While this might be the obvious part of the plan of action, I believe that not enough people are speaking the truth. Not online, but publicly. With the rising tide of political correctness, I can already see people in public quickly receding at the risk of being socially outcast. Appeasement under political correctness seems to be the cultural trend when it comes to handling the truth. This is quite worrying, as the more we capitulate, 'truth' becomes subjective through group-think, not individualism. What *they* say, will eventually be the 'truth'. Don't let this happen.

Don't worry about hurting people's feelings by speaking the truth. We've been doing it for hundreds of years, and we've managed to get along fine without the 'thought police' banging down our doors. If someone publicly speaks falsehoods, correct them. Be tactful, but concise. If nobody counters with the facts, how do we know it's incorrect? It is your duty to get knowledgeable, to fight deceit. Otherwise, who is else is going to do it? Don't let the media, or even standardised educational books tell you what 'the truth' is. Liberal academics are getting it wrong everyday, but their poison is still becoming a part of the national education syllabus. Thirty years ago, there was a sense of sobriety and probity in education. We weren't conspicuously under attack by insidious and subversive Marxist ideals being funnelled into school. Today, we have climate change fear-mongering, gender non-binary pseudo-science, the academic rejection of only two genders, the demonisation of the middle-class, capitalism, democracy, and the rabid attack on Christianity. This has got to stop, lest we lose our future.

Likewise, do not be afraid to speak up at the risk of losing your social media accounts. Why would anyone want to invest their lives in a system of appeasement, when they, the tech overlords will purge you in the end, regardless? Your dignity is worth more than a few hundred thousand subscribers and followers. Don't take the 'social credit' bait, and the quick, fickle fix of sudden popular fame through a few viral videos. The more we involve ourselves in the system of compliance, it will continue to grow. We are in a cultural war, as I have already stated. Do not give credence to the enemy of the state. Inform the public of their nefarious ways, and resist their agenda at all costs. It is only through disengagement, and negative publicity, that their stock prices will begin to fall. This is the key in bringing the whole wretched system down. If need be, crowd-fund an independent social media platform only for conservatives. While many will prefer to use Gab.ai as an alternative, I could never understand why Andrew Torba founded the platform as a free speech haven for *all* political persuasions, when only liberals are welcome on other networks. This is simply irrational, and counter-productive. The liberal tech elite have shown us the door, handed us our hat and coat, and told us to get out. Why pander to them any longer? Remember, they brought the war to us. When we are welcomed back, then they will be embraced likewise.

An independent, conservative social network platform doesn't have to be elaborate like Twitter or Facebook. Those platforms are very vacuous and self-serving anyway. We are to serve liberty, not liberal trends. Even a Reddit style online forum is still the best way to learn, share and reach out. You'd be surprised that I actually do not gravitate towards social media, but website forums. I still find them far more engaging than vapid social media on the aforementioned networks.

Finally, always stay independent and true to your character. And when I say independent, I do not mean 'liberally progressive and trending'. That is herd mentality. You were born an original, don't die a copy. The reason being is that, for obvious reasons, liberals hate independence, and thrive on group-think, cliques and social conformity. Take it away from them, and they're lost. Natural individuality is an affront to Marxism, because the system cannot control you when you're completely independent in thought and character. They're afraid your influence will inspire other people to rebel against the system. The only person you can truly rely on is yourself.

Likewise, in an age where the youth, and even the middle-aged, are dabbling in tattooing, all I can say is think twice. Tattooing does not equal independence and individuality. The ink culture suddenly came about during the Obama years, which was intended for the west to get physically marked for governmental tracking. In reality, the tattoo culture derives from herd mentality. It's a form of social servitude to the cultural Marxist system. And we all know why cattle get either branded, or tattooed - because eventually they end up being slaughtered, like the Jews in the death camps, who were also tattooed.

Don't be that person. Live free, die hard.

GET COMMUNICATING

It's inevitable that unbridled, conservative voices on the internet are going to become a thing of the past. But it's not over yet. There's a little thing called the post box. They're not ornamental. They still work. We're forgetting that we still have a postal service that can never discriminate, due to privacy. Before the rise of the internet, people still communicated via post. And before you scoff at the idea, you'd be surprised to know that paper and letters actually are more effective than vapid, deletable emails. There is nothing worse for a senator or congressman or woman to receive the cold hard facts on paper, through registered post. Moreover when it's written by a legal team or organization.

I find emails to be very impersonal. A hand written letter is more valuable, professional and effective than any email can ever be. Therefore, I would strongly encourage all to get communicating, the old fashion way. It's worked since 1775, and so far, it hasn't let us down. Getting back to basics means you're untouchable from the prying hands of Big Tech. Running conservative mail campaigns are far more likely to draw engagement. Think about it. Are you more susceptible to retain the information on a printed paper addressed to you, or the email that gets lost with the dozens of others in your inbox? Moreover, it isn't that costly to get a club established for conservative readers. I find email to be overrated. Don't get me wrong, it's convenient. But people receive too much these days for your voice to stand out. Even if it's not junk mail, it just appears to be. This is why traditional mail can work to your advantage. In fact, online printing companies are incredibly cheap these days. Printing off a few thousand leaflets, including postage costs, is very cheap.

You'd be surprised how many corporations started their humble roots like this. As they say, 'The pen is mightier than the sword.' The liberals might seem to own the internet now, but they're cannabalizing. Thus is the problem with implosive cults. Recent news already report that internal conflicts at Google have begun, where witch-hunts are running rampant to persecute liberals who might share conservative news, only for reference. The hysteria will only continue for so long, until the system crashes. I look forward to that day. Use their chaos as your own opportunity while you can, and start a new retro style form of rebellion against the tech overlords. They can shut you down online, but they can't stop the postal system. Enjoy this privilege, before they start registering mail based on your national i.d.

KNOW THY ENEMY

This one is a no brainer, but I cannot stress enough the importance of studying the mandate of Saul Alinsky. One cannot begin to fight the enemy, lest they understand how the enemy thinks. Alinsky is the sole reason why our society is crumbling into the dystopian mess it is today. He is also to blame for the rabid, radical youth who are seeking to bring America and the west to its knees. After all, it's why Alinsky titled his book "Rules for radicals." It's also no surprise why he dedicated his subversive manuscript to Satan, a.k.a Lucifer, whom the author calls "the first rebel."

As you read his Marxist themed handbook, also pick up a copy of any biography on Obama, and see how Alinsky's method of internal destruction is fitting with the former president's career. Once you see the parallels and similarities in teachings, you can then understand the liberal mind. By understanding your enemy, the communists, you can predict and counter their movements. Finally, you must read the communist manifesto, and recognise the signs in the American political landscape. Things always start small, and then it gets worse. Obama was the worst communist sleeper cell to come to power. Be vigilant, be prepared. Educate your neighbours, friends and acquaintances. Communism is coming to America, and it's our job to prevent it from taking a permanent foothold in this great land through education.

OPPOSE NEO-COMMUNISM AND THE SHARIA

I cannot stress enough that it is imperative all patriots resist and oppose any green deal the liberals try to sneak in, or push for their 'sustainable energy' goals, no matter how innocuous. Indeed, the latter sounds like a great opportunity, but believe me, our governments never do anything to benefit the public first. There's always a catch. Nothing is green-lit until it serves the elites' agenda of world-wide control.

What is a certainty, is that green deals will lead to a monopoly on battery powered energy, where gasoline generators, combustibles, all used for independent living, will be banned. These insidious eco-deals have absolutely nothing to do with protecting the environment, or 'climate change', but controlling people under the UN's Agenda 21 scheme. The goal is to push everyone on to a battery powered grid, through mass taxation of agricultural, rural land. Just like in soviet Russia, the government will place people in 'affordable' accomodation, city apartments, where they will be controlled and spied on. This is not far-fetch. It's happened before through sheer demagoguery, and it's happening again. The government is already spying on us. Heck, even Trump was spied on by Obama.

It's a fact that people are becoming more dependent on city living for work, which is creating dystopian slums. The UN's Agenda 21 manifesto is centred around 'regionalization', which is another term for district style, prison cities. Of course, the elites will live on the higher ground, while us peasants will be subjected to a soul-crushing, sterile life of conformity, only existing in their shadow. In the coming future, for those who are deemed 'hateful', i.e non-compliant, they will have their energy cut off for speaking up against the tech tyranny and government negligence. If said individual persists, the corporate-government will turn off the entire district to motivate citizens to hunt down, and punish the dissident. It's quick, cost-effective, and wholly devious. Yes, you heard correctly - corporate-government. Mark my works, the government will certainly hybridise itself with private corporations. It's already happening now, as Obama worked closely with Big Tech for his agenda, and we can see Trump hardly lifting a finger to stop the gang of four, despite them ostensibly working against him. This is how the state will persecute people and get away with it, through corporate indemnity.

Finally, it is also certain that liberals will continue to allow Sharia law to spread in the west, as it is aligned with their principles of draconian control. Local imams will play an important role in autonomously ruling over districts through force, which gives the government time to breathe, and enjoy the fruits of their labours. Certainly, we are heading into a neo-pharaoh system of oppression. And remember, all of this started with censorship.

Be warned.

MY FINAL WORDS

If you have digested even a fraction of what I have written in this book, you will know now that we are heading into dangerous territory. These are very disturbing times. The Bible calls it 'The End Times', others, 'the fall of western civilisation.' Whatever *you* call it, you must understand that the freedoms you took for granted today and yesterday will not be there in the coming years. There is a contagious, maddening sense of liberal hysteria in the world. Witch-hunts are on the rise, and the line between common sense and sanity is quickly diminishing. It is evident that liberals are becoming drunk with power, and will stop at nothing until they virtually kill their enemy. As you have seen from the aforementioned genocidal quotes by the elites, they don't even consider us equal, or human. We are to be exterminated, for we have not earned the right to live in their coming new world. They have already designed the plans, and indeed we are already being silenced.

This is fascism defined. And cunningly, fascism has come to the west in the guise of progressive liberalism. In reality, it's our own fault. We should have seen the signs, especially when we warned years ago by people such as former president Ronald Reagan.

> "If fascism ever came to America it would be in the
> form of liberalism."
> - President Ronald Reagan

But you see, liberals do not see themselves as fascists, but 'revolutionaries', as Google's *The Good Censor* document purports. It is thus that we have seen the rise of liberal militancy, cloaked in social activism called ANTIFA (Anti-Fascists), and other hardline leftist groups. Again, we should have seen what was coming, especially when Churchill himself warned us of the reverse psychological tactics that the enemy of liberty would play on us.

"The fascists of the future will be called anti-
fascists."
- Winston Churchill

Churchill, was indeed a smart leader. But above all, he was not afraid to be called a patriot, and a nationalist, who believed in fighting to the last man to defeat real fascism. Today, those who stand up against the beast, or are proud of their country, are labelled as 'hateful racists', 'white colonialists', or 'uncle Toms'. The latter insults have been all too often used against the wise, regardless of their race, who have woken up to how leftists predominantly use Islam as a battering ram to bring down the west.

What we have learned over the last ten years, is that Islam is indeed the bullet in the liberals' gun, for it is wholly incompatible with western law, democracy and the constitution. Churchill knew this all too well. If he was alive today, there is no doubt he would be enemy of the liberal state for his memoirs contained within the book, *The River War*. As a soldier in WWI, he was privy to the decaying infrastructure, and stagnation in Islamic countries. Moreover, he saw how Sharia systematically oppressed the people, specifically unbelievers, as it reduces them down to the mere level of a worm. Even back then and today, Islam is synonymous with liberal fanaticism, indolence, and arrogance. Thus the two ideologies work hand in hand. Again, it's our own fault that we didn't heed Churchill's warning of what Islam does to any country it festers in.

"How dreadful are the curses which Mohammedanism lays on its votaries! Besides the fanatical frenzy, which is as dangerous in a man as hydrophobia in a dog, there is this fearful fatalistic apathy. The effects are apparent in many countries. Improvident habits, slovenly systems of agriculture, sluggish methods of commerce, and insecurity of property exist wherever the followers of the Prophet rule or live. A degraded sensualism deprives this life of its grace and refinement; the next of its dignity and sanctity.

The fact that in Mohammedan law every woman must belong to some man as his absolute property, either as a child, a wife, or a concubine, must delay the final extinction of slavery until the faith of Islam has ceased to be a great power among men. Individual Moslems may show splendid qualities - but the influence of the religion paralyses the social development of those who follow it. No stronger retrograde force exists in the world. Far from being moribund, Mohammedanism is a militant and proselytizing faith. It has already spread throughout Central Africa, raising fearless warriors at every step; and were it not that Christianity is sheltered in the strong arms of science, the science against which it had vainly struggled, the civilisation of modern Europe might fall, as fell the civilisation of ancient Rome."

Remember, the globalist goal is to usher in order out of chaos. Wherever Islam spreads, chaos ensues. Even though Churchill's book was written over a hundred years ago, until now, Islam has not changed. As the former prime minister predicted, we are now seeing the fall of civilisation as we know it; and it's all because of liberalism. The orchestrated invasion of Syrian migrants, and the planned takeover of the west was unashamedly manipulated by the Democrats, and left-wing alliances in Europe.

Islam's incompatibility with the west, which has always been foreseeable to be a dangerous liability, is the reason why the religion was banned in American under Theodore Roosevelt's administration. You see, back then, our leaders bore some semblance of common sense, as they knew the dangers inherent in the Muhammadan faith. Little did they know that the cult would be exploited today for a Marxist agenda to bring down patriotism, by ushering in hate speech laws. Nonetheless, where the term 'patriot' has become part of the conservative lexicon of late, it will be very telling to see how Trump actually addresses the situation of diminishing free speech and Big Tech tyranny. As I have already mentioned, there is already a growing sense that he may be controlled opposition, but I hope it's not true. In the next four years, we will certainly find out. This time is crucial. This is not just any other presidency. Trump holds the keys to our future, as American culture, tech and prowess is the cornerstone of the west. If America falls, we all fall. If the presidency idly stands by while Big Tech ravages our lands, and diminishes our liberties, then we can kiss the future goodbye.

THE ELEVENTH HOUR

For any liberal reading this, don't think that you're safe because you wear the rainbow emblem, embrace Islamic culture, or follow weekly, fickle leftist trends. Your Marxist overlords will come for you next, where your head will be on the chopping block. For in a global, communist world, nobody is safe. The rules change everyday, and the elites will do anything to test the loyalty of the party by placing people in personally-challenging situations. Today, you might be the darlings of the liberal world, but you will also face the same persecution as we have. What is most frustrating, is that you are the reason why the west is failing, and you can't see it through self-delusion and mania. Take a look at the world around you. You're killing your own children through trendy abortion programs, you're emasculating men, persecuting white people, attacking the soldiers who defend you, buying into climate hoax scare-mongering, praising the de-platforming of people based on their politics, you've redefined the word 'racist', bought into Nazi politics, believe that there are more than two genders, and have created an environment of 'guilty until proven innocence'. This is what your children are inheriting, if there are children in the future at all. For just one moment, stop and look at what you're doing. When the world goes belly up, you only have yourselves to blame.

For everyone else, I implore you to be vigilant and be mindful of the little changes occurring in your society. As I said, our governments never do anything unless it benefits them first. There is always an angle to their deeds, and once you recognise this, you will see where the future is taking us. My advice is also to be prepared for society to ostracise you, permanently. The worst thing in the world is betrayal, and believe me, expect to be hung out to dry by your closest. When it happens, it won't be a big shock. These are dark divisive times, and you will be persecuted if you choose truth over conformity. We are living in a day and age where we are seeing our political representatives either compromising on their beliefs, or being shown the door for holding their ground. Don't be surprised when this happens en masse.

As I look at the world slowly imploding, I can't help but think about the millions who have selflessly given their lives to protect our freedoms. Today, all that is left of them is a white tombstone in a military cemetery. How can I possibly visit a war memorial today, and softly whisper to the souls we've lost that their deaths have not been in vain? I would be lying. We have failed them egregiously. I wonder if the young men who willingly gave their lives for a higher ideal called 'freedom', would they be so eager to spill their blood for today's generation who can't tear themselves away from their smart phone, to give just one minute of silence and remembrance in the whole year?

AS I PUT MY PEN DOWN

For everyone who has supported me, the countless emails I have received from people who value what I've done, I thank you. You have truly been an inspiration, and I am humbled by your praise and well-wishes. To those so-called advocates of free speech who have ignored my plea to unite to fight the scourge of censorship, I am truly disappointed. I expected better. I can see now that inherent pride is prominent in conservative circles too. I must say that those who I thought were on my side, but inevitably ignored by pleas, also played a part in censoring me through ostracisation.

As book publishing is becoming ever more constrictive, and social media is completely controlled by the gang of four, I see no reason to futilely continue my quest at this point. Until the internet is free once again, my voice is disappearing into the void. It all rests on our current presidency, and the promise given to uphold free speech. That being said, I have fought the good fight, and I will continue to keep fighting until the last echo dies out, anonymously of course. However, I'm afraid until major change occurs in giving back our freedom, this will be my last publication.

It's been a wild ride, and enlightening to say the least. As I put my pen down, I want to say, take care every one of you. Thank you for all your support. Never forget to seize the day, and always speak the truth. You were born an original, don't die a copy. Live free, die hard.

Sincerely,

J.K Sheindlin

www.ingramcontent.com/pod-product-compliance
Lightning Source LLC
Chambersburg PA
CBHW060458290526
45791CB00001B/172